"Les and Leslie Parrott are two of the most gifted and engaging communicators I know. They understand real relationship issues and offer highly practical and proven advice. This dynamic book will encourage, equip, and inspire you to build relationships you never imagined possible. It's a must read and sure to be a classic relationship resource."

Alan Loy McGinnis
Author of *The Friendship Factor*

"The Parrotts not only have all the facts and figures, the experience, and the background and degrees, but most important, they possess wisdom and compassion. Along with skillful counseling, this book displays a kind and gentle understanding."

Michael Card
Singer and Songwriter

"The authors have done a masterful job of discussing what seldom gets discussed—and must be discussed—by Christians. Anyone trying to help young people should read this book."

Dr. Tony Campolo
Eastern College

"Few people of our time are better qualified to empower us in relationships than Dr. Les and Dr. Leslie Parrott. You will be deeply moved and informed by the biblical principles and strategies that they provide on relationships."

Lori Salierno
Speaker and Author of *Designed for Excellence*

"Les and Leslie have an obvious passion for teaching others to build healthy relationships. They have developed a practical, yet cutting-edge approach, which will help you see the difference between a good relationship and a great one."

Dave Dravecky
Outreach of Hope

"The Parrotts provide a wonderful road map to the marriage relationship that is clear and concise, creative, and incredibly helpful. We're very enthusiastic about this book."

Dr. Clifford and Joyce Penner

Resources by Les and Leslie Parrott

Books

Becoming Soul Mates
Getting Ready for the Wedding
Love Is
The Love List
The Marriage Mentor Manual
Meditations on Proverbs for Couples
Questions Couples Ask
Relationships
Relationships Workbook
Saving Your Marriage Before It Starts
Saving Your Marriage Before It Starts Workbook for Men
Saving Your Marriage Before It Starts Workbook for Women
Saving Your Second Marriage Before It Starts
Saving Your Second Marriage Before It Starts Workbook for Men
Saving Your Second Marriage Before It Starts Workbook for Women
When Bad Things Happen to Good Marriages

Video Curriculum—ZondervanGroupware™

Relationships
Saving Your Marriage Before It Starts
Mentoring Engaged and Newlywed Couples

Audio Pages®

Relationships
Saving Your Marriage Before It Starts
Saving Your Second Marriage Before It Starts
When Bad Things Happen to Good Marriages

Books by Les Parrott III

High Maintenance Relationships
Life You Want Your Kids to Live
Seven Secrets of a Healthy Dating Relationship
Once Upon a Family

Books by Leslie Parrott

If You Ever Needed Friends, It's Now
God Loves You Nose to Toes (children's book)

relationships

How to Make Bad Relationships Better and Good Relationships Great

Drs. Les & Leslie Parrott

ZONDERVAN™

GRAND RAPIDS, MICHIGAN 49530 USA

Relationships
Copyright © 1998 by Les and Leslie Parrott
Workbook Copyright © 1998 by Les and Leslie Parrott
Book and workbook also published in separate editions.

Requests for information should be addressed to:

Zondervan, *Grand Rapids, Michigan 49530*

Library of Congress Cataloging-in-Publication Data

Parrott, Les.
    Relationships : how to make bad relationships better and good relationships great
/ Les Parrott III.
        p.   cm.
    ISBN 0-310-24266-5 (softcover)
    1. Man-woman relationships. 2. Interpersonal relationships. 3. Interpersonal
communication. I. Parrott, Leslie L., 1964– . II. Title.
HQ801.P339   1997
646.7'7 — dc21   97-50106

All Scripture quotations, unless otherwise indicated, are taken from the *Holy Bible: New
International Version*®. NIV®. Copyright © 1973, 1978, 1984 by International Bible Society. Used
by permission of Zondervan. All rights reserved.

Interior design by Sue Vandenberg Koppenol

Printed in the United States of America

03 04 05 06 07 08 /❖ DC/ 10 9 8 7 6 5

*To our students and colleagues at Seattle Pacific University.
You've enriched the past decade of our lives
with countless rewarding relationships.*

Contents

Acknowledgments

So many people have helped us with this project, but it would have never evolved without the synergy and excitement of our friends at Zondervan while sitting around a large conference table on a snowy February day in Grand Rapids. As always, Bruce Ryskamp, president and CEO of Zondervan, has been a supporter whose kindness makes publishing a delight. Our good friend Scott Bolinder, the publisher at Zondervan, is a living example of what we have tried to write about in this book. His vision, authenticity, and integrity make our relationship with him among our most treasured.

We too often take our editors, Sandy Vander Zicht and Lori Walburg, for granted, but we owe both of them a huge debt. The detailed attention and care they give our written words is only outdone by the attention and care with which they treat us as friends.

John Topliff, Greg Steilstra, and the rest of our marketing team have invested countless hours in creative brainstorming on this project and many others for us. We are grateful. We also appreciate the artistic touch of Jody Langley and the time she devotes to packaging our message. Then there is Joyce Ondersma, a woman who goes beyond the call of duty to make our relationship with everyone at Zondervan pure pleasure. We will never be able to say thank you enough to the people of Zondervan who help make our dreams a reality.

Several people in various locales were kind enough to read portions of this manuscript and offer personal or professional commentary and insight. A special word of thanks in this regard is owed to Timothy Clinton, Gary Collins, Jay Jackson, Jeff Joireman, Mary Anne Kaveckis, Jeff Keuss, Kathy Lustyk, Ken McGill, Steve Moore, James Scott Smith, Les Steele, Amy Wagner, Connie Wible, Jacqueline Wilding, and Norman Wright. They each volunteered their time and honest opinions. And this book is the better for it.

Molly Long, Barb Hancock, Dan Benjamin, Gina Dosier, and Amanda Wood assisted us in tracking down more information than any authors have the right to ask for. The value of their collective research skills has proved incalculable for this project.

Few people believe in our message more than Janice Lundquist. Her friendship and professional savvy have helped us spread the word in ways we never dreamed. (Not to mention the deep-dish pizza deliveries during our layovers at O'Hare.) We are blessed by knowing Janice.

Finally, we want to express our appreciation to the hundreds of students at SPU and the thousands of individuals around the country who have allowed us to teach them a few of the basics of building better relationships. To be part of your journey has been an honor.

Les and Leslie Parrott
Seattle, Washington

Introduction

Our Longing
for Belonging

*There is no substitute for the comfort
supplied by the utterly taken-for-granted relationship.*

— Iris Murdoch

Recently a pioneering band of researchers studied the age-old mystery of what makes people happy. Their answer is not what you might expect. What appears consistently at the top of the charts is not success, wealth, achievement, good looks, or any of those enviable assets. The clear winner is relationships. Close ones.[1]

Nothing reaches so deeply into the human personality, tugs so tightly, as relationship. Why? For one reason, it is only in the context of connection with others that our deepest needs can be met. Whether we like it or not, each of us has an unshakable dependence on others. It's what philosopher John Donne was getting at when he said so succinctly, "No man is an island." We need camaraderie, affection, love. These are not options in life, or sentimental trimmings; they are part of our species' survival kit. We *need* to belong.

Not long ago, we spent a Saturday evening on a radio talk show in Chicago. The show was an open line to much of the nation. The two of us sat with a host in a small glass booth full of electrical equipment, and outside a sole telephone operator managed six working lines. From 8:00 P.M. until 10:00 P.M. we talked to strange voices coming from

Anywhere, USA. The lines were never free, always one speaking, five waiting. The subject was relationships, and the calls ranged from questions and opinions about family and friends to sex and romance.

This wasn't so much an interview. We were simply facilitators of a large-scale discussion—adding our two cents' worth when the host wanted a professional sound bite. Once the program got rolling, most of the callers phoned in to commend or clobber a previous caller. "That last guy who called about his mother being so domineering needs to get a life," said one typical caller. "If he doesn't want a meddling mom, he needs to move out of her house." Blah, blah, blah. Having never done a radio show quite like this, we were getting the feeling that most people were more interested in hearing themselves talk than anything else. At least we felt that way before Tom, a desperate college student, phoned in.

"You're on the air, Tom, go ahead," the host said.

"Ya. I've never called a radio station or anything, but I'm kinda ..." Tom cleared his throat and continued speaking slowly. "I'm kinda ..."

"Do you have a question or comment, Tom?" said the time-conscious host. "Go ahead."

"I don't have a question or anything"—deep sigh—"I'm just listening and I feel ... I don't know. . . ."

The host rolled his eyes at us and gave the phone operator on the other side of the glass partition nonverbal signals to get Tom off the line and go to the next caller.

"You called for a reason, Tom," I (Les) said. "What is it you are feeling?"

"Well, it's just that I haven't talked to anyone for so long."

"You haven't talked to anyone!" the host blurted out.

"I've talked to people, but not really talked in a way that means anything."

The host looked quizzical and nodded in our direction.

"So what is it you are feeling, Tom?" I asked.

There was an exception-
ally long silence before Tom
answered with a single word:
"Lonely."

> Intimate attachments to other human beings are the hub around which a person's life revolves.
>
> —John Bowlby

Something about this
word and the way he said it—
his frankness and vulnerability—as well as the follow-up discussion,
drastically changed the tone of the remaining minutes of the program.
The crusty callers and opinionated commentaries seemed to vanish.
One caller after the next echoed Tom's emotion. On this Saturday
night, all over the country, if only for a few minutes, faceless people
phoned in to share the experience of being alone. Even the cynical host
warmed up a bit and wondered out loud: "Aren't all of us, even with
people all around, susceptible to loneliness?"

The answer is yes. In a culture where we can pull money from a
machine and never interact with a human bank teller, walk on a
crowded sidewalk without meeting another's eyes, and call telephone
assistance only to get information from a computerized voice, it's truly
possible to be alone in a crowd. National surveys, in fact, find that a
quarter of all Americans say they've felt lonely in the last month.[2] And
if they don't confess to feeling lonely, two-thirds of Americans say that
having close relationships with other people is always on their minds.[3]

Surprisingly, college students—living with attractive, intelligent,
pleasant people—are among the most relationally-starved members of
society. The number-one reason college students seek counseling, in
fact, is for their relationships.[4] Some experts explain this by saying students tend to be overly idealistic, expecting too much from potential
mates and friends. Others say students may reject possible friends and
partners because they're overcome with their own social anxiety and
fear of rejection. Whatever the reason, everyone agrees that no matter what our age, we all have a deep longing for belonging.

We want to be wanted, accepted, enjoyed, and loved. Psychologists call it our "affiliative drive." And make no mistake, no one is too

big, strong, talented, or tough to go without belonging. The need to belong is not just about feeling warm and accepted, however. It's literally a matter of life or death.

A LIFE OR DEATH ISSUE?

During World War II, doctors identified a fatal and mysterious disease they called marasmus. It was discovered in a group of orphaned babies who were placed in a care facility with brightly colored toys, new furniture, and good food. In spite of the pleasant accommodations, however, the health of these children rapidly deteriorated. They soon stopped playing with the new toys and gradually lost their appetites. Their tiny systems weakened, becoming lethargic and wearing down. Some children died.

When word got out, United Nations doctors were flown in to make a diagnosis and treat the children. After only a short time of investigation, the doctors made a simple prescription, curing the problem within days: For ten minutes each hour, all children were to be picked up by a nurse, hugged, kissed, played with, and talked to. With this simple prescription, the little ones brightened, their appetites returned, and they once again played with their toys. Their "marasmus" was cured.[5]

Unfortunately, this incident was not the first to link the importance of human relationships to our very survival. In the mid 1700s, Frederick II, King of Prussia, conducted one of the grizzliest experiments ever done. He wanted to prove that newborns, if left unattended except for the provision of food and water, would begin speaking Latin on their own. Needless to say, the babies perished.

As infants, we do not know or understand the subtle dynamics of relating and love, but our need for connection is already so strong that its absence impairs natural growth and development, even bringing on death. This profound and deep human need for nurturance does not change as we grow older. Not by a long shot. Adults who isolate themselves from the world, refusing so much as to own a pet, are likelier to die at a comparatively young age than those who cultivate companionship.

> Happiness seems made to be shared.
> —♪ Corneille

Two independent studies, one done at the University of California at Berkeley and the other at the University of Michigan, found that adults who do not cultivate nurturing relationships have premature death rates twice as high as those with frequent caring contact. James S. House of the University of Michigan said, "The data indicates that social isolation is as significant to mortality as smoking, high blood pressure, high cholesterol, obesity, and lack of physical exercise."[6]

THE COMPLEX COMPANY YOU KEEP

Social scientists call our longing for belonging assimilation, affiliation, or social webbing. Others call it fellowship, connecting, or relating. Whatever it's called, everyone agrees that we're born with an insatiable inner need for meaningful interaction with others. It's a need that begins on the first day of our lives and continues until we take our last breath.

So make no apology for your strong desire to be intimate with someone. Don't ignore the need by preoccupying yourself with surface satisfactions. Everyone wants to be wanted, accepted, enjoyed, and loved. Neglecting your longing for relationship by claiming to be above it is as foolish as pretending you can live without food. Our need for relationship is all part of God's design.

If our need to belong, to find intimacy with others is so universal and even ordained, you may be wondering, *why is it so complex? Why is it sometimes so difficult?*

We wonder the same thing. Relationships can be downright complicated. For starters, our own family, the people we love the most, hold the potential for causing us the greatest pain. And who hasn't experienced the puzzle of a relationship where flourishing affections faded without warning? The friends we trust the most sometimes fail us the worst. Then there's the mystery of relating to the opposite sex. Need we say more?

You'd think that after all the time we humans have had on this earth, we'd have made negotiating our relationships a little more simple. It's not that we haven't tried. But even our folk wisdom on relationships raises more questions than it answers. Do birds of a feather flock together, or do opposites attract? Does absence make the heart grow fonder, or is out of sight out of mind?

No doubt about it, in spite of all our good intentions and sincere efforts, relationships are rarely simple. A good indication of the complexity of modern relationships, according to comedian Jerry Seinfeld, is that greeting-card companies are forced to put out cards that are blank on the inside: "Nothing—no message. It's like the card companies say, 'We give up, you think of something. For seventy-five cents it's not worth us getting involved.'"[7]

Well, as educators and counselors who have studied many of the intricacies of human relationships, we can't give up. And through this book, we've decided to get involved. Not that we want to meddle in your relationships. It's just that after years of serious study and countless counseling sessions, we have our hands on some of the most cutting-edge strategies, skills, and insights for nurturing healthy relationships. They are principles that can help you solve many of your relationship problems before they even begin. And through this book we want to pass them along to you. We don't pretend to answer every question you have about relationships; we don't even promise to make your relationships more simple. But we do intend to make your relationships healthier, happier, and stronger.

READING THIS BOOK FOR ALL IT'S WORTH

Before we hit the road, let's get ready for the journey. A quick overview of this book will help you see where we are headed. We begin in chapter 1 with who you are and what you bring to your relationships. Unless you have a heightened awareness of your relationship readiness, you are likely to end up caring more about the *dream* of being in a relationship than about the *person* you are in relationship with. The first chapter sets the course for all those that follow.

In chapter 2, we'll show you how your family of origin, for better or worse, continues to impact your present-day relationships. We'll also show you how to use your family tree to your advantage so its influence doesn't rub against your grain.

Chapter 3 is dedicated to bridging the gender gap. Here, you'll learn to speak the language of the opposite sex and discover whether or not men and women can be "just friends."

Next, we take a serious look at friendship. Chapter 4 explores the ins and outs of making friendships that last, while chapter 5 will show you how to make the best of a bad situation: when even your good friends fail you.

The next three chapters will cause you to face your love life—head on. We'll begin in chapter 6 by revealing the secrets to finding the love you long for, while chapter 7 will mince no words about the sometimes dicey subject of sex. Since nearly everyone who dates eventually experiences a breakup, chapter 8 will show you how to handle this often painful situation with integrity, whether you are the "heartbreaker" or the "brokenhearted."

We'll conclude our journey with an exploration of the ultimate relationship, sometimes so mystical, so ethereal, it's overwhelming. Bypassing pat answers, chapter 9 will help you relate to God—without feeling phony.

One more thing. Throughout each of these chapters you will find a number of places directing you to personal exercises in the *Relationships Workbook*, which is located at the back of the book. It contains dozens of practical self-tests and assessments you can complete in just a few minutes. They are designed to help you go beyond just reading this book to internalizing and applying its content.

> Human relationships always help us to carry on because they always presuppose a future.
>
> —↯ Albert Camus

Before you read the first chapter of this book, it is our hope that your relationships are already growing strong. But by the time you come to the end of this text, if you have stayed the course, we believe you will have the tools you need to make bad relationships better and good relationships great. We wish you every comfort and blessing healthy relationships bring, and we pray you will never take them for granted.

chapter one

The Compulsion for Completion

It is only when we no longer compulsively need someone that we can have a real relationship with them.

—⌁ Anthony Storr

In the autumn of 1992, we did something unusual. We offered a course at Seattle Pacific University that promised to openly and honestly answer questions about family, friends, dating, and sex. In short, its purpose was to teach the basics of good relationships.

Colleges around the world offer instruction on nearly every conceivable topic, but try to find a course on how to have good relationships and you'll look for a long time. We wanted to change that. As a psychologist (Les) and a marriage and family therapist (Leslie) teaching on a university campus, we had our hands on stacks of relationship research showing that, with a little help, most of us can make our poor relationships better and our good relationships great. And that's exactly what we wanted to teach students to do.

The course was to be an informal group with voluntary attendance; any student could be present or drop out at any time if he or she so desired. We called the class "Relationships."

Our determination to start such a class was met with no resistance from the powers that be, as long as it was taught free of salary and on our own time without load credit. Of course, a few eyebrows were raised by those who considered relationships neither a scholarly subject nor a serious part of a university curriculum. We were amused in the ensuing weeks by a few odd looks from some colleagues. One professor in discussing our plans called the course "Irrelevant!" Others asked mockingly if the class had a lab requirement.

Nevertheless, the course was offered that autumn, and students enrolled. After the first day of registration, we received a call from the registrar's office informing us that our classroom, big enough for twenty-five students, had been moved to an auditorium, where we were forced to close enrollment at 225 students. We've been teaching the course, the largest on our campus, ever since.

Since that first autumn, we have lectured on campuses and in churches across the country, teaching the basics of good relationships. And we always begin with the same sentence: *If you try to find intimacy with another person before achieving a sense of identity on your own, all your relationships become an attempt to complete yourself.*

This single sentence holds the key to finding genuine fulfillment for every relationship. If you do not grasp its message, the best you can hope for is a false and fleeting sense of emotional closeness, the kind that comes from a series of temporary attachments. Once the truth of this sentence is understood and internalized, however, you'll discover the abiding comfort of belonging—to family, friends, the love of your life, and ultimately God. A solid sense of who you are provides the foundation you need to forge friendships that last and to find your soul mate.

> Each man must have his "I"; it is more necessary to him than bread.
>
> —✒ Charles Horton Cooley

Let's be honest. Many of us at some time in our lives have felt as though something is missing. All of us have struggled with loneliness. We've all felt detached, unaccepted, separated from the group we'd like to be part of. And when we find ourselves in this empty space, we typically search outside ourselves—often compulsively—for something or someone to fill it. We shop, we drink, we eat, we do anything and everything to distract ourselves from the pain of feeling alone. Most of all, we tell ourselves, *If I find the right person, my life will be complete.* Too bad it's not that simple. If it were, we'd have friends that never failed us and marriages that never fractured. The truth is, the cause of our emptiness is not a case of missing persons in our lives, but a case of incompletion in our soul.

In order to build healthy relationships, you must be well on your way to becoming whole or complete. You must be establishing wholeness, a sense of self-worth, and a healthy self-concept. And this chapter will help you cultivate it.

You can think of this chapter (and the exercises in the workbook) as your guide to exploring the secret contained in the single sentence: *If you try to find intimacy with another person before achieving a sense of identity on your own, all your relationships become an attempt to complete yourself.* This chapter will guard you against the deadly lies that sabotage potentially good relationships, and it will show you the ins and outs of achieving a healthy sense of identity or self-worth. The journey begins, however, with a look at our innate hunt for wholeness.

THE QUEST FOR WHOLENESS

Stephanie, a student in her mid-twenties, came to our office to talk about her current relationship, the third in a series that had each lasted almost a year. This one was with Dan, an older, confident college grad. She was nearly trembling with happiness as she spoke about their relationship.

> Love consists in this, that two solitudes protect and touch and greet each other.
> —Rainer Maria Rilke

"I'm so in love with Dan," she told us. "Last weekend he gave me this adorable little teddy bear to celebrate our ten months of dating." She went on to describe his good qualities. "He's amazing; I just hope . . ." Stephanie's chin started to quiver and before she could finish her sentence, she was crying. I (Leslie) handed her a box of tissues and asked her what was wrong. She wiped the tears from her eyes and blurted out that she was terrified of doing something wrong and "ruining it."

"I've done it before," Stephanie confessed. "I get in a relationship, things go pretty well for a while, and then I do something to mess it up."

"Like what?" Les prodded. "What might you do that would make Dan leave?"

Stephanie, still sniffling, confessed her fears of being stupid, irresponsible, lazy, or just about any other undesirable trait she could think of. She told us that she always feels better about herself when she's dating a guy. "It's like I'm somehow more complete," she said.

Les looked at me with knowing eyes. It was obvious. We'd heard this same story with different names and faces many times before. Stephanie was riddled with insecurity and desperately afraid of losing her boyfriend because, for the time being, he was what was giving her a sense of self. By being attached to Dan, Stephanie felt more whole.

"I'd do anything for Dan," Stephanie volunteered.

"Maybe that's the problem," Les boldly replied.

Stephanie looked surprised, but at the same time, inquisitive. The rest of our session was spent holding up a figurative mirror to help Stephanie see what she was doing. Like an anxious child dreading a parent's departure, she was trying desperately to avoid a slip-up that would cause her boyfriend to leave. With Dan and all the rest, Stephanie was more concerned about pleasing her partner than she was about building a relationship. Why? Because, like everyone else lacking a solid sense of personal wholeness, she was looking to another person to complete her identity. No wonder she was terrified of a breakup.

The human quest for completion can be overwhelmingly powerful, yet it generally doesn't operate at the conscious level. It does its work below the surface and drives us into believing some of the most lethal of all relationship lies.

●◦ Exercise 1: Your Relational Readiness

Socrates was right. Every once in a while it's good to take a deep breath, undergo evaluation, and "know thyself." We all need objective feedback now and then. And when it comes to assessing what we bring to our own relationships, most of us need all the help we can get. This first exercise in the *Relationships Workbook* is a self-test that will help you identify your own compulsion for completion.

LIES THAT SABOTAGE OUR RELATIONSHIPS

The pioneering sociologist George Herbert Mead was known for saying, "The self can only exist in relationship to other selves."[1] In other words, having a relationship, being a member of a community, helps us discover who we are. We couldn't agree more. But while relationships are the path to discovering the self, they do not guarantee the development of a *complete* self. That's the rub. If we have not achieved a solid sense of who we are on our own, we are destined to believe one of two subtle lies guaranteed to sabotage all our relationships: (1) I need this person to be complete, and (2) If this person needs me, I'll be complete.

I Need This Person to Be Complete

By attaching ourselves to another, according to this first lie, we become instantly whole. Complete. All our needs are met. Case closed. The enticement is too much for the needy to resist. Who can pass up a short-cut, as it were, to personal growth? No wonder so many drink its poison.

Rebecca sure did. In her late twenties, she was a study in misery. She'd dated Tom a few times in college, but nothing serious ever developed. A few years later, a job brought Tom back to Seattle, where he and Rebecca attended the same church and began to pal around. "We're more than friends," is the way she described it. "You could say we're dating, but the sparks aren't really flying, at least for Tom." She talked about how Tom was focused more on his career in marketing than his relationships. In fact, he was now considering a move to Kansas City to enroll in a training program that would make him more attractive to potential employers. That's what brought Rebecca to our office.

After four months of quasi-dating in Seattle, Rebecca was considering a move to Kansas City to be with Tom. "My job is nothing to brag about," she told us, "and I have an aunt in KC who said I could stay in her spare room for a while."

I (Les) thought I might be misunderstanding and asked for some clarification: "You're going to move halfway across the country to be near a guy that has made no commitment to your relationship?"

"I know! Isn't it crazy?" Rebecca said with nervous excitement. "But Tom and I were made for each other; he just doesn't know it yet.

> The desire for approval and recognition has been one of the major driving forces throughout my life.
>
> —Hans Selye

It probably doesn't make much sense, but it's something I've got to do. I mean, something could really develop between us."

I winced inside, knowing how much she longed for a relationship and how potentially painful such a decision could be. We explored other options for a few minutes, but she wasn't interested. She didn't want advice. Rebecca was headed to Kansas City—following her relocated knight in shining armor—and there was no talking her out of it.

Have you ever seen a scenario like this? It's not unusual. When people buy into the myth that another person will meet all their needs, they will do almost anything—quit their job, change their appearance, have sex, get pregnant, or travel to the ends of the earth—just to be with them. People who believe another person will complete them by meeting all their needs become human chameleons. Remember Zelig from the Woody Allen movie of the same name? He became who everyone around him wanted him to be. He was externally defined, looking to others to tell him who he was. People who believe this lie do the same thing. The problem is that chasing after another person to have a relationship that makes you feel better about yourself spells certain disaster. And Rebecca's situation was no exception.

Six months after her move, Rebecca showed up again at our office door. "Hey! I thought you were in Kansas City," Leslie exclaimed.

"Not anymore," said Rebecca. "Things didn't work out so well." For the next thirty minutes Rebecca told us how after only a few weeks, Tom began dating another woman he met in his training program, and they were close to getting engaged. She said she was doing all right, but since she had "lost" Tom, she was lowering her expectations and "settling" for guys she would have never considered previously. Before leaving our office that day, Rebecca spent at least thirty minutes tearing Tom apart.

Too many people attach themselves to another person to obtain approval, affirmation, purpose, safety, and of course, identity. And when the inevitable disappointment happens, they complain bitterly that this person failed them.

The truth is, self-worth does not come from the mere existence or presence of someone in your life. When you come to a relationship lacking personal self-worth, all you can

> know thyself.
> ⌐ Inscription on the Oracle
> of Apollo at Delphi, Greece
> (6th century B.C.)

offer is neediness. And even if you do win the heart of another, you'll still, over time, come up empty. That's the poison of this lie. Expecting another person—whether it be a friend, a dating partner, or your husband or wife—to provide you with your life is unrealistic and actually unfair. It isn't anyone else's job to give you an identity or make you whole. People in your life are meant to *share* it, not *be* it.

If This Person Needs Me, I'll Be Complete

The second relationship lie is just as lethal as the first, but more cruel. The person living this lie appears to be less desperate. They aren't contorting themselves to win the approval of another. Instead, they are seeking someone simply to win. Operating out of the same vacuum of personal identity and self-worth, they want a relationship with someone—

anyone—who will build up their weak ego. They aren't interested in commitment, only conquest. And the more conquests, the better.

For believers of this lie, a person becomes an object to acquire, like a shiny prize with bragging rights. What they feel about the person they are dating doesn't matter as much as what they feel about themselves when they are with their date. Their attitude demonstrates hedonism at its height. And it shows little respect for others.

We recently attended a play at the Seattle Repertory Theater to see Rex Harrison reprise his famous role in the

> Love is not possessive.
> —⌁ 1 Corinthians 13:4 (NAB)

classic musical, My *Fair Lady*. The play begins with Professor Henry Higgins standing on a London street. Next to him is his old friend Colonel Pickering, and they're looking at the third character, Liza, a flower girl, a street urchin. The two men talk back and forth and make a gentleman's wager to see if Professor Higgins can turn the flower girl into a princess. Higgins spends long hours teaching Liza proper English and proper mannerisms. The test of his teaching comes on the night of a large social event. Liza, in a fancy gown, is presented as a princess—and people believe it.

At home later that night, Professor Higgins is out of the room and Liza is sitting with Colonel Pickering. She's reflecting on what's happened in her life. "I've finally figured out the difference between a flower girl and a princess," she says. "It's the way people treat you. And 'enry 'iggins treats me like a flower girl. For him, I'll always be a flower girl."

The people buying into this second lie—"If this person needs me, I'll be complete"—are like Professor Higgins. For them, a person is just another project, an accomplishment to put on their relationship resumé. They don't have to respect the person; just being needed by the person is enough to make them feel better about themselves, at least for the moment.

And if you're thinking the believers of this lie are simply shopping around for a person to care for, they're not. What they really care about is the dream of having others care for them. It's just that they don't realize that in trying to make their dream come true, they have to make huge compromises. Let's face it, when your goal is to be needed, you're not going to attract the healthiest of people. Any generic boyfriend or girlfriend will do.

At twenty-seven years of age, Rick, a meticulous dresser with a healthy physique and an easy smile, had dated more women than he could count. He was active in two different singles groups at local churches, and his reputation as a "lady's man" was wearing thin. By the time I (Les) met him, he was exploring the idea of "settling down."

The setting was a picnic table at a retreat where Leslie and I were the speakers. Rick was telling me about Tina, his most recent catch. "I don't know what to do," he said. "She's nice and everything, but she's not—oh, I don't know."

"She's not what?" I prodded.

Rick was struggling to find the words. "It's time for me to get serious and all, but Tina?" he asked as he rolled his eyes. "I don't think so."

"You mean she's not ready to get serious?"

"No, no, no," Rick laughed. "She'd get serious in a second. It's just that I don't think she's the one."

"Why not?"

"That's the thing, I don't know why not."

We continued to talk for a while at that picnic table and later in the dining hall. We never did reach a resolution. I'm not sure Rick ever will, at least until he figures out that another woman, no matter how much she needs him, cannot complete him.

Rick, like every other believer of this lie, will be stymied by true love until a sturdy sense of self-worth and wholeness is established. And that's an inside job that depends on nobody but oneself.

HOW TO BECOME WHOLE

If it's not already crystal clear, we'll say it plainly: There are no short-cuts to personal growth and wholeness. If you try to complete

> I suppose everyone continues to be interested in the quest for the self, but what you feel when you're older, I think, is that . . . you really must make the self. It is absolutely useless to look for it, you won't find it, but it's possible in some sense to make it.
>
> —⚡ Mary McCarthy

yourself through another person before you establish a sense of self-worth on your own, the best you can hope for is an illusion of wholeness. And it's a quick-fading illusion at that.

So, you ask, *What can I to do to get whole?* That's a great question. And if you're serious, it means you're ready to sidestep the fairytale belief that the right person can make your life complete. It also means you need a plan. The remainder of this chapter is dedicated to helping you find your way to personal wholeness. We do not pretend to have the answer for everyone, for each person's journey to wholeness is unique. But we know from personal experience and the wisdom of others that people who become whole learn to (1) heal their hurts, (2) remove their masks, (3) sit in the driver's seat, and (4) rely on God.

These four steps will take you farther than you think. The test of your determination, however, will be the first one. It's the toughest.

Heal Your Hurts

I (Les) never thought I had any "hurts." I pretty much sailed through my school years and even college without many jolts. Relative to others, I've never had any right to complain. But during my first year of graduate school I suffered a relational bruise I didn't expect. A friend, someone I was close to, did an about-face. He was suddenly no longer interested in our friendship. *What did I do?* I wondered. I reviewed our relationship, our conversations, but nothing made sense. Out of the blue, it seemed, he suddenly had no time for Les Parrott in his life. To this day, I'm not sure why. It was painful, for sure, but something I knew I could survive. Or did I?

As part of my clinical training, I was in counseling. And it seemed like a pretty good place to find resolution to this perplexing problem. But as I recounted the story, I had no idea what it would lead to. It stirred all kinds of feelings. Then and there, my trusted counselor had me explore my personal history and look only for moments of abandonment. I didn't like this idea and wondered, *What's this have to do with my friend's behavior?* As it turned out, nothing. It had to do with me and healing any residue of pain in my past.

The exercise, at first, seemed silly. Most of the memories were just normal childhood experiences (like being lost in the grocery store) that were terrifying at the time but quickly forgotten. However, my counselor pointed out that, for whatever reason, I still remembered them. The point of this exercise in self-exploration was to help me acknowledge and accept my relational pain—no matter how big or small—instead of burying it. And that's important. I've since learned that repressed feelings, especially painful ones, have a high rate of resurrection. That's why the place to begin your journey toward wholeness is where it hurts.

> We forge gradually our greatest instrument for understanding the world—introspection. We discover that humanity may resemble us very considerably—that the best way of knowing the inwardness of our neighbors is to know ourselves.
>
> —Walter Lippmann

For some people, personal hurts run deep; for others they appear to be mere scratches. Whatever your situation, this step toward wholeness is crucial. Be aware, however, that healing your hurts is a process of painful self-exploration. Personal growth almost always is. But no matter how painful the process, it's worth the price. It's a bit like the Greek myth about the nymph Pandora.[2] Hidden inside the box were all the painful parts of Pandora that she was trying to avoid, the parts she had tried to bury. It was those hidden and buried parts that were giving Pandora trouble. When she first opened the box, all the painful parts came storming out.

This is the part of the story that most of us know, but there's more. As those parts were exposed to the light, as she explored the hidden pieces, she made her way to the bottom of the box, where she found that which had been missing in her life—hope. As she explored all of the hidden pieces, she found her key to wholeness. And the same will be true for you. When you open the Pandora's box within you, you may find painful parts you'd rather ignore, but as you work through them, you will find hope at the bottom of the box just like Pandora did.

You may be wondering why the first step to wholeness is necessary. I certainly did. But I learned that the purpose behind this process is to protect you from repeating the pain of your past in your present relationships. That may sound strange, but the truth is we use new relationships as replacement parts for old hurts and old losses (a parent or an ex-boyfriend or girlfriend, for example).

Every relationship, in a sense, gives you another chance to resolve issues you didn't get squared away in a previous one. But if you do not heal your hurts, you'll never get them squared away. You'll just continue to repeat relational problems and replay your pain again and again. And when this pattern develops you'll have created a much bigger problem. You will no longer relate to people, but only to what they represent. In other words, the new person in your life will not really be the object of your feelings. It will be what he or she symbolizes—an opportunity to work through the issues you had with someone else.

Get the point? This first step is vital to your personal growth. If you take the time to explore your personal pain (see Exercise 2), you will have set the foundation for wholeness and will be on your way to having genuine relationships . . . assuming you take off your mask.

➣ Exercise 2: Healing Your Primal Pain

Whether you believe you have hurts to heal or not, take a moment to explore any pain from your past and how it may impact your present relationships. This exercise in the *Relationships Workbook* may be one of the most important things you can do to keep from repeating painful patterns in your life.

Take Off Your Mask

"You're the first person I have ever been completely honest with."
Every psychologist hears these words from time to time, but it was Sidney Jourard who made sense of them in his in-depth book, *The Transparent Self*. He was puzzled over the frequency with which patients were more honest and authentic with a clinician than they were with family or friends. After much study, he concluded that each of us has a natural, built-in desire to be known, but we often stifle our vulnerability out of fear. We're afraid of being seen as too emotional or not emotional enough, as too assertive or not assertive enough. We're afraid of rejection.

The result? We wear masks. We put up our guard. We become what Abraham Maslow called "jellyfish in armor" by pretending to be something we aren't. Consider the words of this letter, whose author is unknown, but which could have easily been written by each of us:

> Don't be fooled by me. Don't be fooled by the face I wear. I wear a mask. I wear a thousand masks—masks that I am afraid to take off; and none of them are me.
> Pretending is an art that is second nature to me, but don't be fooled. For my sake, don't be fooled. I give the impression that I am secure, that all is sunny and unruffled within me as well as without; that confidence is my name and coolness my game, that the water is calm and I am in command; and that I need no one. But don't believe me, please. My surface may seem smooth, but my surface is my mask, my ever varying and ever concealing mask.

The writer goes on to confess that underneath the mask is no smugness, no complacence, only confusion, fear, aloneness, and sheer panic at the thought of being exposed. Then this piercing paragraph:

> Who am I, you may wonder. I am someone you know very well. I am every man you meet. I am every woman you meet. I am right in front of you.[3]

Why do all of us hide behind masks? We vacillate between the impulse to reveal ourselves and the impulse to protect ourselves. In a seemingly inexplicable paradox, we long both to be known and to remain hidden. Why?

One reason is that we admire anyone who's calm, cool, and collected. For men, especially, the emotionally inexpressive hero like James Dean, Clint Eastwood, Robert DeNiro, or Ethane Hawk presents a self-reliant and tough image we want to emulate. The primary reason we wear our masks, however, is to guard against rejection. *If people knew the real me, they'd never accept me*, we say to ourselves. So we slip behind a self-made facade and pretend. Sociologists call it impression management; the rest of us call it pain.

If we wear our masks long enough, we may guard against rejection and we may even be admired, but we'll never be whole. And that means we'll never enjoy true intimacy. Here's the situation. When what you do and what you say do not match the person you are inside—when your deepest identity is not revealed to others—you develop an incongruent or fragmented self. Your outside doesn't match what's going on inside. You're consumed with the impression you're making on others, constantly asking *What should I be feeling?* instead of *What am I feeling?* You're always wondering what other people think of you. You walk into a relationship and ask yourself *How am I doing?* instead of *How is this person doing?* And that subtle shift from thinking of yourself to thinking of others will move you into authenticity, a defining quality of wholeness. Congruent people have the security to focus on how others are doing—not because they want to look good, but because they genuinely care.

Does the whole person never wear masks? Of course not. When we encounter potential rejection or harsh evaluation, we need an occasional mask to save face. Allow us to tell you a secret every congruent person knows. Most of the time, with most people, vulnerability begets vulnerability. Once you take off your mask and reveal the real you—your fears, your desires, your excitement—others are likely to do the same. It's disarming to learn you're not alone. Vulnerability, you could say, is what builds a bridge from one person to another.

So if you are ever to achieve personal wholeness, it will be because you have the courage to drop your guard, take off your mask, and be real. It will be because you risk rejection from another to be true to yourself.

➡ Exercise 3: Taking Off Your Masks
All of us wear social masks (acting calm or confident when we're not) from time to time to protect us from rejection. This exercise in the *Relationships Workbook* will help you discover just what your masks look like and when you are most likely to wear them.

Sit in the Driver's Seat

It's so easy to be passive—to move through life simply reacting to outside forces. Like passengers on a bumpy bus ride, we watch the scenery flash by our window as life happens around us. We show up, sit back, and let fate determine our destination. It's been said that most of us plan more for a Christmas party than we do for our lives.

And when it comes to achieving wholeness, to building a solid sense of identity and self-worth, we want something to happen to us. Like magic, we want to be zapped with an insight, with wisdom, or even a mystical experience that will change us. The problem is, you don't catch a sense

> *An humble knowledge of thyself is a surer way to God than a deep search after learning.*
> —Thomas à Kempis

of self-worth from reading a book or attending a seminar or seeing a therapist. Self-worth comes from hard work. It is earned. It comes from dreaming to make a difference and then making the sacrifices to make your dreams a reality. Wholeness is forged from your efforts. You will never achieve it as a mere passenger; you must sit in the driver's seat. In his play *Don Juan in Hell*, George Bernard Shaw correctly concluded: "Hell is to drift, heaven is to steer."

Taking responsibility for your destiny will determine the kinds of relationships you build. People without a growing sense of wholeness, without responsibility, have hellish relationships. They behave more like beggars than choosers. Consider the dating game. It seems that even some species of the animal kingdom have more relationship savvy than we humans. When it comes to choosing a mate, for example, a female penguin knows better than to fall for the first creep who pulls up and honks. She holds out for the fittest suitor available. The Asian jungle bird Gallus is just as choosy. And so is the female scorpion fly. But when it comes to human relationships, it often seems that very little effort goes into selecting and choosing. Why? Because we lack initiative, purpose, and clear-cut goals.

All of your relationships, if they are to be healthy, must be predicated on your having an identity, forging a purpose, having courage, and making commitments to things outside yourself. Once you take an active role in the quality of your own life, other people share in your growth rather than becoming responsible for it.

If you are serious about writing your own destiny, however, you will need a couple of tools. To begin with you'll want a personal statement of purpose and a small set of meaningful goals. Your purpose will set your course and your goals will serve as your road map to being the person you were meant to be.

Some of the most advanced corporations make a practice of "revisiting" their mission statement every few years. They study the document that sets forth their original aims and then measure their performance. At regular intervals companies look at whether the aims of the business have fallen out of sync with its mission statement, whether these aims need to be brought back into line, or whether the statement itself needs to be rewritten to reflect current realities. As individuals, we need to do the same thing. A purpose statement keeps us on track. How do you write a personal purpose statement? The workbook exercise for this section will help you here, but you basically have to answer for yourself as honestly as you can: What do you really want from life? Once you determine this, you can craft some specific goals that will help you achieve your purpose.

All the goals in the world, however, mean nothing if you do not have the stick-to-itiveness to make them materialize. If you are serious about taking responsibility for your own life, therefore, you will also need to master the art of delayed gratification. In his compelling book, *Me: The Narcissistic American*, psychoanalyst Aaron Stern gets right to the point: "To attain emotional maturity, each of us must learn to develop . . . the ability to delay immediate gratification in favor of long-range goals."[4]

Are you familiar with the "marshmallow test"? In the 1960s, Walter Mischel of Stanford University ran an experiment where he would make a proposal to four-year-olds: "If you'll wait until after I run an errand, you can have two marshmallows for a treat. If you can't wait until then, you can have only one—but you can have it right now."[5] This was a challenge sure to try the patience of any child. Amazingly, some children were able to wait what must surely have seemed an endless fifteen to twenty minutes for the experimenter to return. To distract themselves, these children covered their eyes, sang songs, played games with their hands and feet, or even tried to fall asleep. And as promised, these plucky preschoolers received the two-marshmallow reward. The children who couldn't control their impulse for immediate gratification, however, grabbed the one marshmallow, almost always within seconds of the experimenter's leaving the room.

Which of these choices a child makes reveals more than you think; it offers a quick read not just about character, but about the course of that child's life. Years later when these children had graduated from high school, it was discovered that those children who grabbed for the single marshmallow were more troubled and tended to have fewer desirable personal qualities. In adolescence they were more likely to be shy, indecisive, easily upset, stressed, resentful, and prone to jealousy. On the other hand, those who had resisted temptation at four were now, as adolescents, more socially competent, embraced challenges instead of giving up, and were better able to cope with the frustrations of life. They were more confident, trustworthy, and dependable. Bottom line, they were reaching their goals.

We like the definition best-selling author Scott Peck gives to delaying immediate gratification. He says it is "a process of scheduling the pain and pleasure of life in such a way as to enhance the pleasure by meeting and experiencing the pain first and getting it over with."[6] Some people learn to schedule pain and pleasure early in life; others must learn this process later in life. Whether you are in the group of early- or late-learners doesn't matter. The point is that if you are going to achieve a sense of wholeness, you are going to have to set goals, and if you are going to meet those goals, you are going to have to delay the impulse for immediate gratification. It's essential to crafting your own destiny.

� Exercise 4: Designing Your Destiny
Writing a personal statement of purpose is not as difficult as you might think. This exercise in the *Relationships Workbook* will guide you through a step-by-step process for discovering your purpose and creating goals that will help you fulfill it.

Rely on God

The final step toward achieving wholeness is one that many fail to take. They may do everything we have discussed so far in this chapter, but they are not maximizing their potential for healthy relationships until they learn to rely on God—not another person—to meet their ultimate needs.

At the core of each of us is a compulsion for completion so strong that no single human can consistently fulfill it. There are times, glorious moments of intimacy and belonging (with family, friends, or a soul mate), that make us feel complete. But those times are few and far between. They are snapshots we paste into our mental scrapbook to fondly recall and treasure. Unfortunately for some, these moments become the mark against which their self-worth and significance in the relationship is now measured.

Julie, a bright woman in a loving relationship, had unknowingly subscribed to this irrational belief, as did her boyfriend, Jack. They had been dating for more than a year and were thinking about getting married. They showed up at our office, however, because they were each a little nervous. As they recounted fun and romantic times together, their love for each other was obvious and their leaning toward lifelong commitment seemed appropriate. In spite of their love for each other, however, they felt uncertain about their value to the other person. According to Julie, Jack's "obsession" with sports, for example, seemed to take precedence over their time together. And Jack felt that Julie's violin lessons often interfered with time she should be spending with him. After airing their frustrations, Julie finally blurted out, "I just need to know I'm the most important thing in his life before I can make a complete commitment."

"That's the same way I feel about you," Jack exclaimed.

Julie and Jack's scenario is universal, and we reassured them that their thoughts were normal. Every serious relationship, no matter how loving, eventually raises doubts about its endurance because it cannot, nor was it ever intended to, meet all our needs all the time. That's a difficult truth to swallow when you're blessed by a loving family or friends, and especially when you are madly in love, but in your journey toward wholeness, it's a truth that cannot be disregarded.

The heart of the issue here is personal significance. This need is woven into the fabric of our nature, our very being. The desperate need for significance is as real as any physical need we ever experience. And we'll do almost anything to get our need for significance met. Some seek money, prestige, beauty, success, achievements, or fame to satisfy the yearning, but sooner or later all of us look to relationships for a deeper level of personal fulfillment. We dream of a relationship that will complete our need for significance. But like Julie and Jack, we realize that even the most loving human relationship can never consistently quench our deepest need. Ask any married couple. Every husband and wife, no matter how loving and godly, has many times failed to provide what their partner has needed most.

Some time ago we spoke at a conference in Singapore. Between sessions, we had time to commiserate about jet lag with fellow speakers Larry and Racheal Crabb. Larry has written numerous books we've long appreciated, and before our waiter had even poured water in our glasses Les had him talking about *The Marriage Builder*, a book we felt Larry had written just for us.[7]

During the first year of our marriage, this book uncovered a secret neither of us wanted to face. It showed us how we were counting on the other person to make us feel significant. At an unconscious level, Les was saying, "I need to feel important, and I expect you to meet that need by respecting me no matter how I behave and by supporting me in whatever I choose to do. I want you to treat me as the most important person in the world. My goal in marrying you is to find my significance through you." Leslie had a similar unconscious message: "I have never felt as deeply loved as my nature requires. I am expecting you to meet that need through gentle affection even when I'm in a bad mood or not being sensitive to what you need. Don't let me down."

> God loves each of us as if there were only one of us.
>
> —Augustine

It was hard to swallow, but it was true. We desperately wanted the other person to consistently and unfailingly meet our deepest needs for significance even though it was an impossibility, a desire no human could meet.

So are we stuck, forever floundering between fleeting moments of relational fulfillment? Fortunately not. While our earthly relationships will let us down time and time again, a relationship with God can be counted on to genuinely and fully meet our deepest need for significance. As we will see more clearly in the final chapter of this book, only God can ultimately and consistently love us when we are moody, when we make mistakes, and when we feel rejected and unloved by the person we counted on the most.

"God is love." And we can rely on God's love. As the writer of the Psalm said, "My flesh and my heart may fail, but God is the strength of my heart."[8] The New Testament says, "God lives in us and his love is made complete in us."[9] Once we internalize this truth, we discover the ultimate cure for our compulsion for completion. We may heal our hurts, discard our masks, and even take ownership for our destiny, but ultimately, only God's love can make us whole.

FOR REFLECTION

- What do you make of the idea that it is only when we no longer compulsively need someone that we can ever attempt to build a healthy relationship with them? Do you agree? Why or why not?

- Of the two lies discussed in this chapter which do you encounter more often: (1) I need this person to be complete; or (2) If this person needs me, I'll be complete?

- How willing and comfortable are you to disclose yourself to others and let yourself be known by others? What social masks do you sometimes wear that guard you against being vulnerable? When are you likely to wear them?

- On a scale of one to ten, how would you rate your current tendency to delay immediate gratification? If you do this well, what's your secret? If you are striving to do this better, how can you improve?

- It's easy to rely on another person instead of God to meet your deepest needs. Why do you think most of us struggle with this idea?

chapter two

Keeping Family Ties from Pulling Strings

Sometimes you'll get so far away from your family you'll think you're outside its influence forever, then before you figure out what's happening, it will be right beside you, pulling the strings.

—Peter Collier

I (Leslie) will never forget the day my mom reported me missing. It started like any other day when I was in kindergarten, with one exception. As she helped me get dressed we rehearsed a plan, a "serious" plan I was to follow: Immediately after school I was to walk home, let myself into the backyard, and play there until she came home. Mom was almost always home for me when I returned from school, but on this day she and Dad both had unavoidable appointments, leaving me home alone for a few minutes that afternoon.

The day at school passed agonizingly slow as I rehearsed the plan in my mind. When the final bell rang, I hurried home, eager to please Mom by following her instructions. But just as I stepped onto the sidewalk in front of my house, Mrs. Magee, our next-door neighbor, came running. "Leslie," she said, "your daddy just called and he wants you to come to my house until he gets home." So I followed Mrs. Magee into her kitchen and played with some dolls while she baked cookies.

As the first batch of cookies was cooling, we heard a piercing siren and ran to the windows. There, next door in my own driveway, was

Mom, frantically waving a photo of me and sobbing as she talked to a police officer. Just then, my father's car came screeching into the driveway. Before I could run to my mother, Dad was explaining that I was safe, that he had made arrangements for me to wait with Mrs. Magee next door.

"Why on earth didn't you tell me?" my mother shouted at Dad. She scooped me up brusquely and carried me inside where she and my dad had the worst fight of my entire childhood. All I could do was stand helplessly by—knowing I was the cause. It was the single most horrifying moment of my first five years.

Who would think that such an early event would have such lasting repercussions? But it did. In fact, it still does. The first time I became consciously aware of how this early event impacted my life was during our second year of marriage. We were living in southern California, going to graduate school. On this occasion, I was to pick Les up at Los Angeles International Airport, something I had never done. And when I arrived at the pre-established spot, just under the United sign, Les was nowhere to be found. I panicked. *I must have misunderstood. He's going to be so upset with me. But he should have been more clear. I feel like such an idiot.* A shower of negative and anxious thoughts came over me. I'm generally an easy-going person who can roll with the punches, but I was losing it.

A few minutes later, Les showed up with a smile on his face like nothing had happened.

"Where've you been?" I demanded.

"Oh, I thought we were meeting on the lower level," he explained.

"Well, I'm never picking you up again!"

"What's wrong?" Les asked, wide-eyed and confused.

I couldn't answer because I didn't know. I just teared up as we circled out of the airport in silence.

This wasn't the first time this seemingly inexplicable anxiety had struck. But it was the first time I ever saw the connection to what happened when I was five years old. As we drove from the airport back home to Pasadena that day, Les patiently and compassionately helped me unpack my feelings (after all, he was studying to be a psychologist!). We talked about other times we'd had minor miscommuni-

> Whoever said that death and taxes are the only inevitable things in life was overlooking an obvious third one: family.
>
> —William J. Doherty

cations that led to painful misunderstandings. And we talked about "the first time" I'd ever experienced these intense feelings. That's when the light went on. For more than two decades, invisible strings had been tied to my feelings and played me like a puppet. The miscommunication I witnessed between Mom and Dad when I was five had left such a powerful imprint on me that any similar situation could trigger an onslaught of needless negative feelings. This phenomenon is what psychologists mean by "emotional baggage," and no matter how healthy our home, we all have it.

How could it be otherwise? No other relationship shapes who we are more than our family. Most of what we think, feel, say, and do is in response to the home we grew up in. On the conscious level, we either buy into or reject the lessons learned from our family. And on an unconscious level, through a kind of osmosis, we absorb ways of thinking, feeling, and being. Either way, we can't escape its influence. From the career we choose to the person we marry, from the politics we support to the values we live by, every conceivable aspect of our lives is influenced by family—whether we know it or not.

Our family is like a classroom where we learn the skills and knowledge that will one day enable us to live outside it. Our families teach us to trust or distrust the people around us, to speak up or stay quiet in a social setting, to give or to take. They teach us what kinds of feelings are acceptable, appropriate, and tolerable. "It is in the family," says Theodor Lidz, "that patterns of emotional reactivity develop and interpersonal relationships are established that pattern and color all subsequent relationships."[1] Did you catch that? Our family sets the pattern for all other relationships.

We therefore dedicate this chapter to understanding the lessons, both conscious and unconscious, you learned at home—and whether those lessons will prove useful in relating to others. By the way, once I understood the connection between my moments of anxiety and the incident of miscommunication when I was five, I was able to dismantle my irrational panic and keep it from wreaking havoc on my relationships. And when it comes to your family ties pulling your strings, you can do the same. So we begin by briefly exploring how your family teaches relationship lessons (both good and bad). We then focus on the "three Rs" your family taught you and how you can use them to your greatest advantage. We conclude this chapter with a special message to anyone whose parents have gotten divorced.

THE COMPELLING POWER OF YOUR ORIGINAL KIN

We all started off in some sort of family. Perhaps yours was the typical American family with 2.3 kids, a mom, and a dad. Perhaps you were raised by your older sister or your grandparents. Perhaps you haven't seen your father for twenty years. Perhaps your mother became both mom and dad to you. Or maybe yours was a blended family with stepbrothers and sisters. Whatever your family portrait, typical or not, it's had a powerful imprint on you since day one. Literally. Learning begins in life's earliest moments and continues throughout childhood.

Consider a baby who wakes up at three in the morning. Her mother hears her crying down the hall and comes in to tenderly comfort and nurse her. For thirty minutes or more the mother holds the baby in her arms, rocks gently back and forth, and gazes affectionately into the infant's eyes. She tells the baby she's happy to see her, even in the middle of the night, and then hums a sweet lullaby. Content in her mother's love, the baby soon drifts back to sleep.

Now consider another newborn who also awoke crying in the wee hours. But this baby is met instead by a tense and tired mom. Earlier that evening she and her husband began a squabble during dinner that turned into a fight just before going to bed. The baby starts to tense up the moment the mother pulls her from the crib. "Come on, kid, let's get it over with," she says in exasperation. As she nurses the baby, the mother stares stonily ahead and mulls over the cross words with her husband. The baby, sensing her tension, squirms, stiffens, and stops nursing. "You got me up for that?" the mother says sharply and abruptly puts the baby back in the crib and stalks out. The baby cries herself to sleep.

These two scenarios are presented in a clinical report as examples of the kinds of interactions that, if repeated over and over, instill very different approaches to life and relationships.[2] The first baby is learning that people can be trusted and counted on to help, and that she can be effective in getting help. The second baby is finding that no one really cares, that others can't be counted on, and that efforts to get help usually fail. Of course, most babies experience a mix of both kinds of interactions. But to the degree that one or the other is typical of how parents treat a child over the years, basic emotional lessons are imparted about how to interact with others.

We were recently invited to the home of a couple who had just installed a brand-new video game for their five-year-old son, Wesley. We sat in

> The shadow cast by the family tree is truly an astonishingly long one.
> —⤳ Maggie Scarf

their living room after dinner so they could show us how it worked. What we saw next, however, revealed more about their family than it did about their new toy.

Wesley started to play while his parents, almost instantly, displayed overly eager attempts to "help" him. "Not so fast, honey. More to the right, to the right!" his mother shouted. Her urgings were intent and anxious. Wesley stared wide-eyed at the video screen, trying to follow her directives.

"You've got to line it up, son," the father chimed in. "It won't work unless you have it in line, and you've got to get ready to shoot." He started to grab the controls from Wesley but then suddenly jerked his own hands away and clasped them behind his back as if to say *I'm not going to interfere.*

Wesley's mom meanwhile rolled her eyes in frustration. "Now, you've got to move it to the left. You're not doing the stick right . . . stop. Stop. Stop!"

Wesley bites his bottom lip and hands the controls to his dad. At this point, Mom and Dad start bickering about how to work the game as Wesley's eyes well up with tears.

They fiddle with the game for a while until the father gives up and tosses the controls to his wife. "Here, you do it," he says. "Hey, where'd Wesley go?"

These are the moments where deep lessons are taught. Not intentionally, mind you. But taught just the same. And what did Wesley learn? Most likely, that he's incapable of doing things himself, that it's hard to please people, and that his feelings don't really matter. All that from a single incident with a video game? Not exactly. But if similar moments are repeated again and again over the course of his childhood (where Mom and Dad are routinely overbearing, raise their voices in exasperation, and lose their patience), a clear and enduring message is sent.

The point is that small exchanges between you and your family had emotional subtexts, and the messages, if left unexamined, will last a lifetime and shape every relationship you try to cultivate. For this reason, we turn next to helping you uncover the unconscious lessons you learned and the unspoken messages they reveal.

●◆ *Exercise 5: How Healthy Is Your Home?*

Every family has a different emotional climate with differing patterns of relating. And while no family is perfect, some are more harmonious and well-functioning than others. This exercise in the *Relationships Workbook* will help you assess your own family functioning and thus determine areas of growth.

THE THREE R'S EVERY FAMILY TEACHES

It would be so convenient if the lessons our family taught were filed in an old family trunk locked away in the attic. We'd lift out a dog-eared journal containing the lesson plans and customized curriculum our parents knowingly and unknowingly used. We'd peruse our personal transcripts to discover the courses we'd unconsciously taken: "Feelings We Don't Talk About in This Family," "The Way We Avoid Arguments," "How We Express and Don't Express Intimacy," "Advanced Blame Shifting," and so on.

Unfortunately, discovering just what you learned from your family is not quite that easy. But it doesn't have to be terribly difficult either. Generally speaking, the lessons you learned from your family are the result of three Rs: (1) the rules they reinforced; (2) the roles they asked you to play; and (3) the relationships they modeled.

Family Rules

Each family has its own unique set of rules. And while family rules may be explicit, they are more often unspoken, operating outside the conscious awareness of every family member. No one may say, for example, "Never ask anyone for help," but the rule is unconsciously articulated and formed from picking up subtle and not-so-subtle attitudes. Hearing family stories about how brave Uncle John was to go it alone or how silly someone else was to have to depend on others, for example, can be a way of saying "you should do the same."

Family rules unconsciously guide individuals by describing what family members should do and how they should behave, even if they fly in the face of a person's real desires.

Julie, an intelligent, enthusiastic woman in the first year of an M.A. program, was dating Steve, who had his sights set on being an actor. Steve quit high school in his senior year to play a few bit parts in some local productions, but he was now struggling to make ends meet while working part-time as a waiter. Julie and Steve had been out about a dozen times, and the relationship was getting serious. Julie loved

Steve's wit and carefree spirit. With Christmas coming up, they were discussing their holiday plans when Julie found herself—without any forethought and almost against her will—blurting out, "I don't think we should keep seeing each other." Out of nowhere, it seemed, she was calling it quits. She was as baffled as Steve, but stuck to her decision. Without explanation, her mysterious proclamation was the catalyst for a very sour breakup.

After the holidays, Julie came to my (Leslie's) office, heartbroken, depressed, and confused. She relayed her story and confessed, "I don't know why I did that. He was a great guy, and now he thinks I'm psycho." The more we pressed for an explanation the more apparent it became that Julie really didn't want to break up with Steve, but for whatever reason, she felt compelled to do so. And this wasn't the first time she'd broken up with someone without a good reason. That's when we began exploring her family history.

As we talked, I asked an exploratory question: "Julie, who among your circle of family and friends is especially invested in your dating decisions?"

"It's funny you should ask that," Julie said. "My father has never expressed interest in the guys I date, but I think he's the most invested. In fact, I'm scared to death he won't approve."

As we explored her family background, it became apparent that an unspoken family rule was at the root of Julie's decision to break up with Steve. Her father was a disciplined, hard-driving physician who ruled with an iron fist. He was kind but reserved, and rarely intimate, vulnerable, or warm. A series of exercises revealed rule number one: "Never confront your father and always, always attempt to please him." A close second was "No matter what else you do in life, get a good education." These unspoken rules may seem obvious to you and me as outsiders looking in, but they were a flash of insight to Julie. All of a sudden she saw why she was drawn to Steve, but at the same time didn't want the relationship to progress too far. She was testing her boundaries with her father. As a young adult she felt compelled to please him but wanted to be her own person too. Once Julie raised her awareness of the unspo-ken rules she was operating by—the rules her family unknowingly per-petuated and instilled in her—she was more able to make conscious, intentional decisions about her life and her relationships. In fact, last I heard, Julie explained her insight to Steve, and they were dating again.

What about you? What unspoken rules does your family live by? Here's a sampling of the ones we hear most often:

- Don't reveal your true feelings.
- Never hide your emotions.
- Always get your point across.
- Never raise your voice.
- Do everything you can to win an argument.
- Compromise whenever you can.
- Trust others only after they've earned it.
- Never call attention to yourself.
- Let others know your accomplishments.
- Put on a happy face.
- Always be genuine.

The list could go on and on, but what really matters is what is on *your* list. Take a moment to think about the unspoken rules your fam-ily lives by and how they continue to influence you. Exercise 6 in the workbook will guide you in this process.

●◑ Exercise 6: Uncovering Unspoken Rules

This exercise in the *Relationships Workbook* will help you become aware of the rules you live by. Once they are uncov-ered, you can then consciously incorporate these rules into your life or choose to transcend them. Either way, your heightened awareness of how your family has shaped you will make your relationships healthier.

Family Roles

Jeff, a twenty-something college graduate came into my (Leslie's) office unannounced. He had been a student of mine a few years back, and I knew he could always be counted on for a little levity.

> Long before birth, even before we are conceived, our parents have decided who we shall be.
>
> — Jean-Paul Sartre

"Hey!" I said as he appeared at my door, "what's the joke of the day?"

"No jokes today, Doc."

Jeff was notably different as we had a bit of idle conversation. Then tears began to well up in his eyes. He dropped his gaze, and we sat together silently for a few seconds. With a deep sigh, Jeff then revealed that his older brother—who was on a fast track in a very successful career—had been recently killed in a car accident. Suddenly, the happy-go-lucky Jeff, who had been content with his retail job at an outdoor equipment supplier, felt the mantle of "oldest and only son" falling on his shoulders. Now that Jeff's role in the family had changed, everything about his future looked different.

Birth order and sibling dynamics are significant factors in shaping one's role in the family. How we act has a lot to do with our family constellation: whether we are oldest or youngest, male or female, and so on. The point is that roles played out within the family, just like unspoken rules, often develop into lifelong patterns of behavior that influence every other relationship.[3]

Before his brother's death, Jeff's role in the family was as a fun-loving, carefree youngest child. But the death of his brother had redefined the boundaries of Jeff's role in the family and created an identity crisis. Suddenly, Jeff looked at all of life differently. His career, his putting off marriage, and his dreams were changing because his perceived role in his family had changed. He now felt much more responsible.

Have you given much thought to your role in the home you grew up in? What part did you play in your family's drama? Consider the following roles to help you more accurately pinpoint your part. Which one comes closest to describing you in relationship to the rest of your family?

- Problem-solver: Always ready with a solution.
- Victim: Pulling compassion and sympathy from others.
- Rescuer: Diving into situations for somebody else's safety.
- Comedian: Ready with a joke for comic relief.
- Mediator: Serving as a bridge between others.
- Confronter: Facing reality and calling it as you see it.
- Healer: Administering healing to emotional wounds.
- Secret-keeper: Holding a confidence tight and safe.

Maybe a label that is not on this list better describes your role. Whatever the case, you may find it helpful to identify other family member's parts. This will help you more clearly define your role. So review the list again and try to determine what role each member of your family played. By identifying your role in the family, you will become more empowered to fulfill it if you choose, or carve out a healthier pattern if need be.

Family Relationships

Perhaps the most powerful method our family has of teaching relationship lessons is by example. "Monkey see, monkey do," as the saying goes. There's really no way around it. We learn how to feel, how to think, and how to act by observing others in our home. And we learn the relationship skills that will either help or hinder the relationships we have as adults.[4] Consider the following.

Ron's mother had a stroke when he was twelve. Her energy was nearly depleted, and she was unable even to dress herself. Ron watched his father support her emotionally and in countless physical ways.

Bethany, fifteen, and Bret, ten, live in a family where both parents find it very difficult to express their emotions. There is virtually no touching between parents and children apart from a brief good-night kiss.

Anthony was raised in a demonstrative family where everyone had the right to be angry, shout, and point a finger. No one really listened or tried to make sense of the outbursts; it was just his family's way of "letting off steam."

Do you think Ron, Bethany, Bret, and Anthony will adopt their family's patterns of behavior? You can almost count on it. Everyone of us grew up in a home where ways of relating were modeled. We absorbed ways of expressing affection and anger, of talking and listening, of burying conflict or resolving it. In short, we absorbed ways of interacting.

> The family is our refuge and spring-
> board; nourished on it, we can advance
> to new horizons. In every conceivable
> manner, the family is link to our past,
> bridge to our future.
>
> — Alex Haley

I (Les) was blessed to grow up in a loving home with lots of care and affirmation. I got along well with my two older brothers, and we always knew Mom and Dad loved each other. But in all my growing up years, I rarely saw Mom and Dad express much affection in public. At home, they might kiss, hug, or hold hands from time to time, but not all that often and certainly not in public.

I never thought about this much until one day when Leslie and I were in college and dating. We were standing in line for dinner at the campus dining hall and she kissed me. Not a quick peck on the cheek. She planted a big smack right on the lips—with people all around! I couldn't believe it. I felt my face turn red and I was mortified, but I didn't say anything at the time. I just laughed nervously and suddenly became concerned about why the food line wasn't moving faster.

Well, you can probably guess what our conversation that night over dinner was about. Kissing in public didn't fit my repertoire of modeled behavior. It wasn't in my family's lesson plans. And as a result, it's taken Leslie and me a while to negotiate the issue. Believe it or not, after more than a dozen years of marriage, I'm still not that crazy about kissing in public. All because Mom and Dad didn't model this when I was growing up? Probably. "We are, in truth," wrote English statesman Lord Chesterfield, "more than half what we are by imitation."

What did you learn about relationships from the models you had at home? What did you learn about expressing affection or resolving conflict? Exercise 7 will help you see just how important your parents' style of interaction is to your own.

•◦ Exercise 7: Lessons Learned from Mom and Dad

A sixteenth century proverb says, "Example is better than precept." No matter how healthy your home, you learned by example and absorbed deficient as well as helpful ways of interacting. This exercise in the *Relationships Workbook* will cause you to take a second look at what you might be taking for granted.

WHERE TO GO FROM HERE

The goal of this chapter is to heighten your awareness of just how powerfully your family has shaped your relational readiness through the three Rs: the rules they reinforced, the roles they asked you to play, and the relationships they modeled. There is a school of thought that says "awareness is curative." And while that may be true in many cases, just being aware of your family's relationship lessons is not always enough to help you transcend them. A pursuit like this runs the risk of two potentially negative side effects, and it's only fair that we point them out.

The first potential side effect is that you would take your new awareness only halfway. That is, that you would recognize the imprint your family legacy has left on your life and then leave it at that. We fear that you might take a helpless stance and allow your background to direct your future, thinking there is nothing you can do about it. Like the old joke about the farmer who sees a man on a horse swiftly galloping by and calls out, "Hey, where are you going?" The rider turns around and shouts back, "Don't ask me, ask my horse."

You can't afford to be like a rider on a runaway horse. Even if you feel out of control, you have everything you need to take the reins and determine your own destiny. You're not helpless. And you are not simply a product of the way you were raised. From here on out, the kind of person you'll be is a matter of perseverance, not parenting.

The other potential side effect is worse than the first. It's that you would blame your family for the lessons they taught or didn't teach. We've seen this far too often. Now, we will readily admit that you may have been ripped off. That your family life could have been a whole lot better. And if you suffered the ravages of physical or emotional abuse, we can't even imagine the deep hurt and pain you feel. We would never glibly brush that aside. Not for a minute. But no matter what kind of family background you had, we guarantee you that chronic resentment and blame will only further entrench the negative qualities you'd like to escape. So we urge you, don't play the blame game. You have too much potential to get waylaid by that saboteur. If you are carrying deep hurts from your family, seek the help of a competent counselor.

The bottom line is that your family—functional or dysfunctional, happy or horrific—is the launching pad for all other relationships. If your home was healthy, count your blessings and pay tribute to Mom and Dad. And if your home was ill, pick yourself up and make a future for yourself without excess baggage weighing you down. Take the good you can and leave the rest behind.

Now, before closing this chapter, there is one more area we feel compelled to cover: How your parents' divorce will impact your relationships. If this does not pertain to you, move on. But if you know the pain of seeing your family self-destruct, we have some encouraging words.

IF YOUR PARENTS GOT DIVORCED

Each year, 1.2 million children see their parents split up. Like high school graduation or getting a driver's license, divorce has almost become an American rite of passage for some kids. Experts say that if

current rates of divorce continue, by age eighteen forty
percent of children will see
their parents divorce.

> Nobody's family can hang out the sign,
> "Nothing the matter here."
>   —⟀ Chinese proverb

If you happen to be one
of these kids, the statistics, no matter how prevalent, are of little comfort when divorce hits your own home. I know. My (Leslie's) mom and
dad split up several years ago, and I am still reeling from the shock. In
the midst of their turmoil I can remember feeling different about my
own relational future. Like I was somehow genetically rearranged
because they, my own flesh and blood, couldn't hold their marriage
together.

After all, studies have found that divorce rates are higher for people
who grew up with divorced parents than for those raised in intact
homes. The reason? Experts point to the unresolved issues adult children have with their parents and how these issues contaminate their
own attempts at connection. With this in mind, we feel obligated to
pass on a few pointers that may help you resolve whatever loose ends
you have about your mom and dad's breakup.

Actually, we are going to give you only one word of advice and
then caution you about three hazards you'll want to avoid. Now for
the advice. Be assured that you are not condemned to repeating the past.
You are not genetically rearranged because your parents divorced. To
overcome the ensnarements this situation might cause, however, you
need to honestly come to terms with the impact their divorce has had
on you. And the best way of doing so is to sit down with each parent,
adult to adult, and ask them to explain why the divorce took place.
Understand that this is not a time for you to judge, correct, or person-
alize their story. It is simply to gather information by hearing each of
them out. If you feel yourself wanting to correct either of them or challenge their perspective, refrain from doing so. Save that for debriefing
with a friend or counselor. Your goal with each parent is to simply hear
their side of the story. Once you understand the divorce from each parent's perspective, you will more clearly see the destructive patterns that

led to it and thus be able to prevent the same thing from happening to you.

Granted, this kind of a talk with each parent will take some restraint, stamina, and courage. But the pain it may cause you in the present will make you and your relationships stronger in the future. It's worth the price.

With that word of advice, allow us to point out three hazards common to children of divorce that are likely to sabotage your relationships if you're not careful.

First, be on the lookout for unresolved anger. You may feel that this issue is settled, that you have expressed your anger in grieving the loss of your intact home, and it is settled. That may be true. But if you ever feel yourself being angry about something or at someone who doesn't deserve your anger, it may be time to reevaluate how you're managing this emotion. When your home life has been fractured, you deserve to feel angry. Anger is not off limits; it's just that you'll want to take special care to keep it from controlling you and your relationships.

Second, beware of conflict-avoidance. After seeing your parents divorce, it is not unusual to run from conflict altogether. You may find yourself burying unpleasant feelings or opinions, for example, because you simply don't want to face the potentially unpleasant consequences. This, of course, is not at all healthy. Genuine, enjoyable relationships require authenticity. And experiencing disagreements or conflicts from time to time does not mean you are doomed to difficult relationships. Quite the contrary. Conflict, when faced squarely and resolved with understanding, can actually deepen your sense of intimacy with someone. So steer clear of conflict-avoidance and take care to be real.

Finally, watch for sagging self-confidence. It is only natural for your self-image to take a few blows in the midst of your parents' divorce. You may have even suffered a serious depression at one time because of it. And even as an adult, the residue of pain from the breakup still remains.

You know it wasn't your fault—that a parent leaves a marriage because of unhappiness with a spouse, not with a child—but you will have times when you feel stigmatized, defective, or even worthless because your family is not together. You can count on it. So be on the watch. Don't allow irrational thinking to creep back into your head and discount your worth.

The past does not have to dictate the present or the future. Studies affirm that those who grew up with divorce can build healthy, happy, and strong relationships of their own. No doubt about it. And coming to terms with the aftermath of your suffering, as well as being on the lookout for issues of anger management, conflict-avoidance, and a sagging self-confidence, are like an insurance policy against repeating the patterns you fear the most.

●◊ Exercise 8: If Your Parents Got Divorced
> This exercise in the *Relationships Workbook* will help you assess how well you are coping with your parents' divorce. It will help you determine areas you may need to be especially aware of as you build your own relationships.

With the first two chapters of this book now under your belt, you have a foundation on which to build some practical relationship skills. In the next chapter we'll teach you how to understand and interpret the language of the opposite sex.

FOR REFLECTION

- Why do you think your family has had more power in shaping your life than any other social force?
- In what specific ways has your family of origin shaped your personality, your career choice, your relationships, your values?
- In what specific ways does your family still "pull your strings"? In other words, how do your early family influences still manifest themselves in your present relationships?

- Of the three major ways families shape us—rules, roles, and relationships—which one do you see as the most influential and why? Can you think of an example to underscore your reasoning?
- If your parents are divorced or you have a friend whose parents are divorced, how do you think that may impact future relationships? Think of both challenges and advantages.

chapter three

Crossing the Gender Line

Because of our social circumstances, male and female are really two cultures and their life experiences are utterly different.

—*Kate Millet*

It's a day like any other when a seemingly normal woman walks into our office, sits in a chair, and says something like, "I don't know what I do to turn men off. Somehow I am pushing them away. Maybe I'm too demanding, or not demanding enough; I don't know. Men are so confusing."

And it could be that very same day in that very same chair that a seemingly normal man, unrelated to the first woman, sits down and says, "I don't get women. I must be doing something wrong or I'd have at least a semblance of a relationship with one of them. Women are so confusing."

We've seen it time and again. Each gender trying to make contact with the other side but becoming dazed and confused in the process. Like an animal who has come too close to a hot-wired electric fence, we've seen both men and women jump back and retreat from the opposite sex because they didn't want to risk the potential pain of misunderstanding or rejection. So they keep their distance.

The barrier between the sexes is built early on in life by our fear of being teased for having a "girlfriend" or "boyfriend."[1] Remember those days? Some researchers can't seem to forget. A classic study of children's friendships has found that three-year-olds say about half

Men and women, women and men, it will never work.

—⋏ Erica Jong

their friends are of the opposite sex; for five-year-olds it's about twenty percent, and by age seven almost no boys or girls say they have a best friend of the opposite sex.[2] These separate social universes reintersect only as the adolescent years approach. Is it any wonder that male-female relationships are confusing?

This chapter is dedicated to helping you—whether male or female—take some of the mystery out of relating to the opposite sex. We don't guarantee to solve the age-old gender puzzle in just a few pages, but we do intend to give you some practical insights for equipping you in your trek across the gender line. We'll help you explore just how different the sexes are, not only in their psychology but in their biology as well, and we will expose the "fundamental cross-gender relational error," an error that will trip you up every time. We then take turns at revealing in detail what women need to know about men and what men need to know about women. Used correctly, you can consider this information your key to crossing the border. Before closing this chapter we do our best to answer the age ol' question of whether or not men and women can be "just friends," free from romantic entanglements and sexual snares.

But let's now begin at the beginning. We start with a straightforward fact: When men and women get together there are, in effect, two worlds—his and hers. The question this raises, however, is what's the difference?

●◦ Exercise 9: What's Your Gender IQ?

Before delving into the bulk of this chapter, take a moment to quickly assess your knowledge of gender differences. This exercise in the *Relationships Workbook* will help you determine how much you already know about the opposite sex—and how much more you still need to know.

A WORLD OF DIFFERENCE

Have you ever wondered why a man can seemingly read a map blindfolded but can't find his own socks? The reason may be found in his genetic makeup. Research is discovering that men and women actually perceive reality differently. In one university experiment, students were blindfolded while an experimenter who served as a guide walked them through a complex maze of tunnels that run beneath campus buildings. After traversing this maze, women were asked to locate a familiar college building. Nearly every woman in the experiment was uncertain and unable to locate it. Men, on the other hand, had relatively little trouble with the task. In spite of all the subterranean twists and turns, men tended to retain a firm sense of direction and with a kind of internal compass were far more likely to identify the location of the building—even after walking through the maze blindfolded. Chalk one up for the male species.

But before you put all your money on men, consider another university experiment. In this one, students were asked to wait in a small room with a cluttered desk while the experimenter "got something ready." The students thought they were simply waiting for the experiment to begin, but this actually was the experiment. After two min-

> The little rift between the sexes is astonishingly widened by simply teaching one set of catchwords to the girls and another to the boys.
>
> —⫯ Robert Louis Stevenson

utes, the student was asked to describe in detail the waiting room from memory. Men, it turns out, didn't do well on the test, and were able to remember very little. Most men were barely able to describe much of the room in clear and accurate detail. They often missed major objects located on a desk right in front of them. Women, on the other hand, could go on and on with precise descriptions of the room's contents. In fact, women proved seventy percent better than men at recalling complex patterns formed by apparently random and unconnected items. One point for the women's side; but who's keeping score? (Actually, the men *are* probably keeping score, but we'll get to that later.)

In these experiments and dozens of others like them, men and women consistently perform at different levels—sometimes men outperform women and sometimes vice versa. Which is all to say that scientists are suddenly fast at work trying to account for the differences, and what they're finding may surprise you.

Why are researchers just now exploring the differences between men and women? The reason can be traced to the 1970s when the feminist revolution nearly prohibited talk of inborn differences in the behavior of males and females. Pointing out distinctions between the sexes was simply off-limits if you were a respectable researcher wanting to keep your job. Men dominated fields like architecture and engineering, it was argued, because of social, not hormonal, pressures. Women did the vast majority of society's child rearing because few other options were available to them. Once sexism was abolished, so the argument ran, the world would become perfectly equitable. But as hard as we tried to squelch our differences, the evidence for innate gender difference began to mount, and admitting the differences between men and women has now become unavoidable. What's more, the differences are not exclusively relegated to how you were raised as a child and society's traditional stereotyping. The differences, research is discovering, may lie much deeper.

> If there is any one secret of success, it lies in the ability to get the other person's point of view and see things from that person's angle as well as from your own.
>
> —Henry Ford

Scientists have not ignored the ol' nature-nurture debate altogether, but they have come to accept that a few fundamental differences between men and women are apparently biological. It turns out that men's and women's brains, for example, are not only different, but the way we use our brains differs too. Women have larger *connections* and subsequently more frequent "crosstalk" between their brain's left and right hemispheres. This accounts for women's seeming ability to have better verbal skills and relational intuition than men. Men, on the other hand, have greater brain hemisphere *separation,* which enhances abstract reasoning and visual-spatial intelligence. Poet and author Robert Bly describes women's brains as having a "superhighway" of connection while men have a "little crookedy country road."[3]

Big deal, you may be thinking, *men can rotate three-dimensional objects in their head and women are better at reading emotions of people in photographs. How's that affect my relationships with the opposite sex?* Fair enough. Here's our answer: If you evaluate the opposite gender's behavior according to your own standards, never considering significant social and biological differences, you will miss out on a meaningful connection because you were compelled to make that person more like you. That's what we call the fundamental cross-gender relational error: assuming that misunderstandings between the sexes have only to do with cross-purposes and not psychological and biological crossed wiring.

Okay, I understand the problem, you are saying to yourself, *but what's the solution?* That depends on whether you are a woman or a man; either way, there are a few things you need to know.

•◆ Exercise 10: What If You Were the Opposite Sex?

Have you ever imagined how your life would be different if you were the opposite gender? Would your career aspirations be different? Would you relate differently to your family if you were the opposite gender? This exercise in the *Relationships Workbook* will open your eyes and help you have empathy for the opposite sex.

WHAT WOMEN NEED TO KNOW ABOUT MEN

If you are a woman reading this book, I (Leslie) want to reveal a few facts that can help you make healthy connections with the men in your life. Not that I have *the* answer on how we women can relate to every man. The male-female connection is too mystical for such claims. But I do have a few insights that have proven helpful to me and many other women. They have to do with knowing how men are different from us. Of course, there are always exceptions to the rule, but generally speaking, here are a few of the important distinctions— the ones that can make or break your ability to cross the gender borderline.

Men are not as in touch with their emotions as we are.

The first problem women run into when they attempt to explore men's emotional needs is that men don't want women to explore their emotional needs. Let's face it women, relative to us, men should come equipped with an emotional thesaurus. I'm not saying they don't feel things deeply, but men certainly don't express their emotions as clearly or as readily as we do. And who can blame them;

> What women want: To be loved, to be listened to, to be desired, to be respected, to be needed, to be trusted, and sometimes, just to be held. What men want: Tickets for the World Series.
>
> — Dave Barry

they were raised that way. Parents, a recent study found, discuss emotions (with the exception of anger) more with their daughters than with their sons.[4] As adults, men naturally tend to have a smaller feeling vocabulary and stuff their emotions. The point? We can't expect men to identify our emotions or their own as quickly as we do.

Men are more independent than we are.

Here's a lesson from "Male Development 101": Very early on, males define themselves in relation to their mothers by being different and separate. Their impulse is to go away and assert their masculinity. Men need to wriggle free, to do male bonding, to place a great deal of emphasis on work (or golf, for that matter) as an escape from being smothered. But it's not so much being smothered by the women in their lives as it is being smothered by their own feelings of dependency. Men need space to be men. And the more fragile a man's sense of self, the stronger the impulse is to flee. So don't expect men to glom on to you and tell you how much they need you. Instead, take comfort in the fact that the men in your life do need you, but most of the time they are trying to deny how much they need you because it poses so many threats to their sense of masculinity.

Men are more abstract than we are.

While you and I are more likely to talk about our fears, feelings, and experiences, men are more likely to talk about ideas, concepts, and theories. Men want to tell you what they know. They use conversation to discover factual information the same way an anthropologist uses a pick and hammer to unearth an artifact. Men gather facts, debate opinions, and solve problems through reasoned conversation. Sociologist Deborah Tannen calls this abstract style of man-speak "report talk."[5] It's well established, so we can't expect men to be too enthusiastic about conversation that serves as a means with no end. We can certainly talk about our fears, feelings, and experiences to the men in our lives, but we can't expect them to listen with the same vigilance we've grown to expect from our girlfriends.

•◊ Exercise 11: A Self-Test for Women Only

If you are a woman, this exercise in the *Relationships Workbook* will help you clarify your thinking and understanding about the men in your life. It will help you more fully discover what women need to know about men.

WHAT MEN NEED TO KNOW ABOUT WOMEN

Now that Leslie has had a say, allow me to turn the tables. Just as there are important insights for women to gain in understanding men, so can you, as a male reader, discover a few tips that will make relating to the women in your life a bit easier. "Every woman is a science," said John Donne. And if we take the time to carefully study women's needs and how they differ from us, we'll discover some fairly universal principles. I'll echo the same qualifier as Leslie, however: There are always exceptions to the rule, but here are some fundamental ways in which women are different from men.

Women are not as independent as we are.

Let's face it: we love the mystique of the rugged "Marlboro Man" image. Sure, it's cliché, but we can't get over this tough-minded, lone cowboy who reports to nobody as he freely rides the range. Women, on the other hand, couldn't give a can of beans about protecting their autonomy. They prize what Harvard's Carol Gilligan calls "a web of connectedness."[6] Just as we are threatened by a challenge to our independence, so are women threatened by a rupture in their relationships. So don't expect women to fully understand and accept your "need for space." Don't expect them to romanticize your independence. Instead, do yourself and your relationships with women a favor—bite the bullet and let them know you value the relationship even when you need to ride the range.

Women focus on the here-and-now more than we do.

Someone defined the future as a place where men spend most of their time. You and I both know that's not exactly true. But it becomes more true in comparison to women. While we are scheming plans and solving problems for a better tomorrow, most women are asking, "What's going on right now and how do I (and others) feel about it?" Women focus on current feelings and experiences because these build emotional bonds of connection between them. So while we men are more interested in the "report" of what has happened and where we are going, women are more interested on building "rapport" right now.[7] The bottom line is that if you want to get down to the task of solving problems for the future with the women in your life, you must first take the time to explore their feelings about the present.

Women are not as competitive as we are.

As little kids growing up, boys play games in large groups, with an emphasis on winning. Competition is the name of this male-gender game. Little girls, on the other hand, play together in small, intimate groups, with an emphasis on minimizing hostility and maximizing cooperation. The same emphasis follows

> The superiority of one man's opinion over another's is never so great as when the opinion is about a woman.
>
> —⫯ Henry James

both genders into adulthood. As men, we still want to prove our point, keep score, and win the debate in conversation, while women are more likely to sacrifice superiority as the price for keeping peace. It's not that one mode is necessarily better than the other; they both have their strengths and weaknesses. But if we want to build a healthy relationship with the women in our lives, we must honor their cooperative spirit and take care not to step on their toes.

➽ Exercise 12: A Self-Test for Men Only

If you are a man, this exercise in the *Relationships Workbook* will help you clarify your thinking and understanding about the women in your life. It will help you more fully discover what men need to know about women.

Making a cross-gender relationship work does not depend solely on recognizing our differences. It's a matter of appreciating those differences as well. Women, for example, can improve their relationships with men when they value the more masculine traits of emotional constraint, independence, and analytical reasoning. And men can improve their relationships with

> It would be a thousand pities if women wrote like men, or lived like men, or looked like men, for if two sexes are quite inadequate, considering the vastness and variety of the world, how should we manage with one only?
>
> —⫯ Virginia Woolf

women when they esteem the more feminine qualities of interpersonal dependence, present-centeredness, and cooperation.

We've known some people who clearly recognize gender differences but then mistakenly try to eliminate them. It's a futile exercise. Gender differences are not eased by creating symmetry—by having men and women thinking, feeling, and doing everything alike. The fact is that men and women *are* different. And people who openly acknowledge their differences *and* appreciate them improve their chances for a successful relationship.

CAN MEN AND WOMEN BE JUST FRIENDS?

We had just stepped off the platform of a college auditorium in Illinois where we were speaking on gender differences. Lingering around us was a small crowd of students who had a few comments or questions. That's when a young, forthright man came bounding up to us and blurted out a question: "Is it possible for men and women to be friends without being romantic?"

The auditorium fell suddenly silent. Even students who were just about out the door turned around to wait for our answer. We mumbled a spontaneous reply that was mostly based on our opinions and then turned the question back on our listeners. "What do you think?" we asked. For nearly another hour we sat on the edge of that platform and listened to a lively discussion while dozens of students gave their two cents' worth.

That was several years ago, but we continue to hear this question so frequently that we would be remiss not to address it before closing this chapter. And since that occasion in Illinois, we have reviewed dozens of scientific studies and surveyed numbers of people about cross-gender friendships to discover whether these relationships can work or not. We've also listened in on countless discussions with men and women on the issue. And believe me, we're now well acquainted with both sides of the argument.

For many people the idea of a man and a woman being friends is charming, but improbable.[8] "It always leads to something else," they argue, meaning that the relationship eventually becomes romantic or soon fizzles out. Perhaps they are right. After all, in contrast to the countless love stories we see in the movies, male-female friendships are rarely acclaimed or depicted as an ongoing, freestanding bond. How many stories can you think of that richly portray or endorse the lasting, devoted friendship of a man and a woman as an end in itself? Even the acclaimed film, *When Harry Met Sally*, which got a lot of people talking about cross-gender friendships,

> When men and women agree, it is only in their conclusions; their reasons are always different.
>
> —∿ George Santayana

ultimately proves to be another tale of romantic love. Billy Crystal and Meg Ryan's tumultuous and endearing friendship is only a stage in the development of the more celebrated attachment of falling in love.

On the other hand, there are those who are seemingly surprised by the question and argue that of course male-female friendships are possible; why wouldn't they be? These people's persuasiveness almost make the romantic pull of such relationships seem unusual. They ignore it altogether. "One of my best friends is a woman," the male proponent of this perspective insists. "And it's never crossed my mind to consider her in a romantic way." Well, that takes care of that, I think. "My friendships with men are far less complex than my relationships with women," a female with this position might say. "We can play sports and just have fun."

In our informal survey of people who are "just friends" with someone of the opposite sex, we heard a number of positive remarks. Over and over, men spoke about how a woman's friendship provided them with a kind of nurturance not generally available in their relationships with men. They said things like, "I don't have to play the macho game with women. I can show my weaknesses to a woman friend and she'll still accept me." When we asked women about their friendships with men, we heard comments like "He is a good sounding board for getting the male perspective, the kind I can't get from my women friends."

Interestingly, women do not report the same level of intimacy as men do with their cross-gender friendships. Even women who count men among their close friends feel barriers between them.[9] Women will say things like, "I have fun with men, and they can even be supportive and helpful about some things, but it's just not the same. If I try to talk to my male friends the same way I talk to my female friends, I'm always disappointed." At first glance the payoff for men seems to be bigger than the payoff for women in cross-gender friendships. But that's not necessarily true. Women report great enjoyment from the diversity their friendships with men bring to their lives.

So does all this mean the answer to the question about men and women being friends is yes? Few relationships issues are that plain and simple. The real answer is "it depends." *So, you say, let's cut to the chase and get to the bottom line: What do these relationships depend upon?* They depend upon how much each person in the relationship is willing to stretch and grow. These friendships, you see, require both men and women to call upon parts of themselves that are usually less accessible when relating to their typical same-sex friends. For a man, a woman friend allows him to express his more emotional side, to experience his vulnerability, to treat himself and his friend more tenderly than is permissible with male friends. What is typically missing for him in this cross-gender relationship, however, is the kind of rough camaraderie he can have with another man. For a woman, friendship with a man helps her express her independent, more reasoned, and tougher side—the harder edge that's kept under wraps in relationships with women. The down side for her is the relative absence of emotional reciprocity and intensity she normally shares with a female friend.

So, okay, twist our arms for a *yes* or *no* answer to this question and the answer will be *yes*. But we will quickly qualify it. Men and women can enjoy friendship together, but not at the same level they do with friends of the same sex. The next chapter, however, will reveal that friendships within our own gender provide tough competition.

FOR REFLECTION

- Consider your cross-gender relationships. What aspects of these relationships with the opposite sex (excluding romantic relationships) seem to be easier than relationships with the same sex? What are the biggest hurdles you encounter in relating with the opposite sex?

- When you were growing up as a kid, what social activities or games do you think influenced your gender roles? Looking back on it, do you put more stock in the way your environment shaped you or the way your biology programmed you?

- This chapter notes several things men and women should know about the opposite gender. What differences could you add either to the list for women to know or for men to know?

- Have you noticed how women use their conversation to build "rapport" while men use conversation to give or get the "report"? What examples of this disparity can you remember from your own experience?

- The major point of this chapter is that we doom our relationships with the opposite sex when we try to change them into being more like us. If this is so, what can you do to accept and even appreciate the different qualities of the other gender?

chapter four

Friends to Die For

The greatest sweetener of human life is Friendship.
To raise this to the highest pitch of enjoyment
is a secret which but few discover.

—⚡ Joseph Addison

I never would have imagined that a thirty-year friendship could begin in a church nursery between two toddlers. But it did. I was crawling in and out of Mrs. Kolskey's lap and playing around her feet when a mysterious new girl appeared in the doorway. From old photos I know that her hair was pulled back into two ponytails falling in ringlets to her shoulders. But in that first encounter, all I noticed was her luminous pair of magenta Mary Janes—the perfect shoes—exactly like mine. My shoes, you must understand, were an all-time favorite birthday present.

So here we were, two girls in deep pink shoes squealing in delight at our commonality. I had found a kindred spirit. Laura was indeed to become the best friend of my childhood, my bunk partner at summer camp, my college roommate, and the maid-of-honor at my wedding. Today, though she lives in Chicago and I'm in Seattle, not a week goes by without a conversation, and not a significant life experience without her support. Laura is truly a friend to die for.

I couldn't have known at age five, of course, how precious this kind of friendship is and how rarely I would find it in my life. But most people do, in fact, find a kindred spirit or two. In fact, only seven percent of people say they don't have someone in their circle of friends who, at any given time, they can rely on as a best friend.[1]

Actually, what most people call their "circle of friends" more closely resembles a triangle. Many people have contact with between 500 and 2,500 acquaintances each year, representing the base of the triangle. Then there are the 20 to 100 "core friends" in the middle. These we know by first name, and we see them somewhat regularly. At the top of the triangle are one to seven intimate friends. These people are closely involved in our lives, and their names are likely engraved on our hearts.

> To the query, "What is a friend?" his reply was "A single soul dwelling in two bodies."
>
> —— Aristotle

This chapter stands as a tribute to friendship and is dedicated to helping you raise your current relationships to their highest pitch of enjoyment and to building a firm foundation for prospective friends in your future. If a friendship is not built on healthy principles, after all, it will not weather the inevitable storms of life—the times you really need a friend. We begin, then, with laying out just what friends are for and how we can cultivate the kinds of friendships that matter most. Next, we explore the ins and outs of how good friendships are made, and then we point to a half dozen qualities you'll need to consider if your friendships are to survive and thrive.

WHAT FRIENDS ARE FOR

Short of torture, society's worst punishment is solitary confinement. In the biblical creation story the Creator, having formed the first person, immediately declared our social character: "It is not good that man should be alone."[2] Most of us, most of the time, would rather be with anyone than be alone. And when we compare being with anyone to being with a good friend, there *is* no comparison. The reasons are endless. Seventeenth-century philosopher Francis Bacon noted two tremendously positive effects of friendship: "It redoubleth joys, and cutteth griefs in half." How true. Friends make the ordinary—running errands or eating lunch, for example—extraordinarily fun. And good friends ease our pain and lighten our heavy load. Bacon had it right, they double our joy and cut our grief. They also strengthen us, nurture us, and help us grow. And without our knowing, they can even save our lives. Literally.

There's exciting news about having a kindred spirit these days. Not only are friends good for the soul but for the body as well.[3] Friends help us ward off depression, boost our immune system, lower our cholesterol, increase the odds of surviving with coronary disease, and keep stress hormones in check. A half-dozen top medical studies now bear this out. Their findings didn't seem to be influenced by other conditions or habits such as obesity, smoking, drinking, or exercise. The thing that mattered most was friends.[4] What's more, research is showing that you can extend your life expectancy by having the right kinds of friends.

Which brings us to a central issue. What are the "right kinds" of friends? What makes a friend "good"? We all know fair-weather friends are no good. These are the people who walk with us in the sunshine, but they are gone when darkness falls. "Wealth brings many friends," noted one wise observer of life, "but a poor man's friends desert him." Overly engaged and emotionally needy friends who don't know the meaning of reciprocity are also a downer. They take and take while we give and give, but we never see a return on our investment. On the other end of the friendship continuum is the know-it-all friend who mothers and smothers with unwanted advice but never asks for our input. In short, friends cannot be your family, they can't be your project, they can't be your psychiatrist. But they can be your friends, which is plenty.

Friendship is a sovereign antidote against all calamities.

—Seneca

Aristotle distinguished three types of friendship: "friendship based on utility," such as eager, upbeat people in business cultivating each other to improve their bottom line; "friendship based on pleasure," like young people interested in partying; and "perfect friendship."[5] The first

> Be courteous to all, but intimate with few, and let those few be well tried before you give them your confidence. True friendship is a plant of slow growth, and must undergo and withstand the shocks of adversity before it is entitled to the appellation.
>
> —⁀ George Washington

two categories Aristotle calls "qualified and superficial" because they are founded on flimsy circumstances. The last —which is based on admiration for another's good character—is much more fulfilling, but also rare. After all, good friends "are few."

The few *good* friends we enjoy generally come in one of two forms, both desirable and equally delightful. They are friends of the road and friends of the heart.

Friends of the Road

Dale was crazy. That's why I liked him. He could always, I mean *always* make me laugh. Whether we were hanging out at the mall, playing pick-up basketball in a park, sitting in Sunday school, or giving serious speeches in Mr. Olson's civics class, a mere glance from Dale could slay me. On more than one occasion I was sent out of the room because I couldn't regain my composure. Dale and I had more in common than hijinks and humor, however. We had countless conversations at all hours of the day and night about everything from pop music to current events to the meaning of life. We also had soul-searching talks about our fears, our futures, our relationships. This was no lightweight relationship. We saw each other through the Sturm und Drang of adolescence. Like two war veterans, we helped each other survive. At journey's end, however, the friendship faded. I haven't seen Dale, my high-school confidant, since the day we graduated.

How does a once-bosom buddy wind up a distant memory? And is a friendship that fades away necessarily a bad thing? I don't think so. There is a line in James Michener's novel, *Centennial*, that speaks to how even good friendships can be fleeting: "He wished he could ride forever with these men . . . but it could not be. Trails end, and companies of men fall apart."

Some friendships are meant to be transitory. Like cowboys who ride herd together for miles, sharing both dusty perils and round-the-campfire coffee, we all have friendships that come to their natural end. Not because of discontent or lack of interest. Simply because the road has run out. We've hit the end of the trail together and it's time to move on to other things, other companies of men.

Understand, these are not failed friendships. Not at all. They are friendships of the road, equally intense, equally necessary, equally worth cultivating and treasuring as the

> Friends are people you make part of your life just because you feel like it. Basically your friends are not your friends for any particular reason. They are your friends for no particular reason.
>
> —Frederick Buechner

long-lasting versions. We couldn't survive without them. They get us through a particular stretch of road, and for that we can be grateful. Sure, I regret not staying in touch with Dale (photos of him still crack me up) and other friends who have shared a portion of my path. I even fantasize about reviving or repairing some bygone relationships. But with most long-lost friends I know I'd have little in common now. Our bond lies in the past, irretrievable except for the memories.

The friends we meet along life's road make the journey joyful. And they are just as fulfilling as friendships of the heart. Well, almost.

Friends of the Heart

Greg. Jim. Monty. Kevin. Mark. Rich. These names sketch out my life, some since childhood. Together, they could tell you more about me than both my brothers. They are my best friends. They are the pals who know my mood swings and my family history. They've watched me soar and seen me fail. Unlike friends of the road, these guys have stayed with me beyond trail's end. No matter how many months or miles intervene, the friendships endure. Our cumulative years of shared biography preserve our connection, propelling us together on the same path. After years of tireless talks we now speak in shorthand.

> Best friend, my well-spring in the wilderness!
>
> —⚡ George Eliot

None of these friends lives near me now, but we rendezvous at weddings and while passing through each other's towns on business. We plan reunions on occasion, and a few of us have recently shared vacations. Sporadic phone calls, as well as e-mail and a few cards or letters here and there, bridge the connection between long lapses. We don't keep up on daily details, but these friends know my headlines and I know theirs. We count on each other and we share an irresistible impulse to keep going, together.

There's nothing like a friend of the heart, long-lasting pals who know us sometimes better than we know ourselves. They bring such comfort to our lives. It's nearly inexpressible. Dinah Mulock, however, describes it pretty well: "Oh the comfort of feeling safe with a person, having neither to weigh thoughts nor measure words, but pouring them all right out, just as they are—chaff and grain together—certain that a faithful hand will take and sift them, keep what is worth keeping, and with the breath of kindness blow the rest away."

Of course, we don't usually determine that a specific relationship will outlast the road. Some do, some don't. That's all, right? Not hardly. In ancient times, friends vowed to be friends forever, no matter what. Maybe you remember the biblical story of Jonathan and David and how

> God gives us our relatives—thank God we can choose our friends.
>
> —⚡ Ethel Watts Mumford

they took an oath to be friends forever. "Jonathan made a covenant with David because he loved him."[6] From then on, when times turned treacherous and their relationship was tested in blood, they banked on one another.

Maybe it would help contemporary friendships stay together if we swore an oath at the beginning, but that's not how most of us become friends. We are more likely to stumble into it by accident. We meet, look each other over, discover that we talk the same language, that we have common interests, and then . . . fate takes over? Not if we genuinely care about the relationship. If we care, we commit. We don't arrange a ceremony or make solemn vows. Most likely, the commitment gradually grows. We commit ourselves to each other, sometimes without even knowing it, in snippets over the long haul, until we find ourselves as committed friends. Looking back, we see we've made a thousand commitments, little ones, again and again, as we had occasion to make them. We never spoke a vow. We just grew into our commitment without thinking much about it. That's the story of friendships of the heart.

With most friendships, new concerns and new faces gradually crowd out the old as we start a new journey. But not with committed friends. They don't flicker and fade; they keep the light on. They are there for the duration and are as elemental to our being as blood to our heart.

Are friendships of the heart more important than our fleeting friends of the road? Not really. We need both. What matters is how a relationship sustains you right now. An achieved friendship—of any brand or bond—is among the best experiences life has to offer.

●◦ Exercise 13: The Friendship Assessment

It's always helpful to get a little objective feedback on the state of our relationships. This exercise in the *Relationships Workbook* will serve as a kind of checkup on any specific friendship that concerns you.

HOW WE FIND TRUE FRIENDS

Friendship is a long conversation. Indeed, the ability to generate good talk by the hour is the most promising indication, during the uncertain early stages, that a possible friendship will take hold.[7]

The pressure to achieve "quality" communication, however, sometimes induces a sort of inauthentic epiphany for overeager friends-to-be (not unlike what sometimes happens with an eager-to-please patient in the last ten minutes of a psychotherapy session). In the first few conversations there may be an exaggeration of agreement, for example, as both parties attempt to connect ("You like sardines on your pizza?! Me too!"). And if authenticity does not enter in soon, the two parties form an uneasy kind of pseudo-friendship that creates more pretense than pleasure. Fortunately, even eager friends do not need to be caught and snagged by this subtle snare. With the proper techniques, they can break free of the pseudo-friendship and achieve true companionship.

The first important technique is to master the art of good talk. This requires just two simple tools. The first is a listening ear. Some people are especially skilled at opening others up. They readily elicit intimacy because they listen well. The late psychologist Carl Rogers called such people "growth-promoting" listeners.[8] His years of research revealed that good listeners *genuinely* convey interest in understanding the other person, they *accept* the person's feelings without interruption, and they *empathize* by trying to see the world from that person's perspective. These are the skills of a good listener: genuineness, acceptance, and empathy.

> People with deep and lasting friendships may be introverts, extroverts, young, old, dull, intelligent, homely, good-looking; but the one characteristic they always have in common is openness.
>
> —Alan Loy McGinnis

Just the other night, a woman charmed me (Leslie) at a dinner party when she wanted to know all about my work at Seattle Pacific University. At first I thought she was simply offering the standard issue question, "So, what do you do?" required upon first meetings. But she wasn't. With her follow-up comments and questions, it became apparent that she wasn't interested in uneasy small talk, she was interested in me ("Sounds like you really enjoy working with students. How'd you catch a vision for that?"). She genuinely wanted to enter my world and understand my feelings; first-rate listeners have a way of doing that. I could have talked to her all night. In fact, I did.

The second tool for creating friendly conversation is self-disclosure. Weighed and measured in appropriate amounts, self-disclosure is the primary ingredient for potential friendship. In fact, no decent friendship can be made without it. Here's how self-disclosure works. You spill something a bit private and chances are something intimate will get spilled back on you. Vulnerability begets vulnerability. Social scientists call it the "disclosure reciprocity effect."[9] Whatever you call it, however, beware: It's risky. If I reveal a part of me, my excitement, my insecurity, whatever, I open myself up to potential rejection. You may not accept what I disclose. You may belittle it or brush it off. If you do nothing less than reciprocate my vulnerability, I feel slighted. But if you do share my secret, if you identify with me, we've struck the cord of friendship and are no longer alone.

C. S. Lewis wrote about the process of self-disclosure and friendship in his classic book *The Four Loves*: "The typical expression of opening Friendship would be something like, 'What? You too? I thought I was the only one'—it is then that Friendship is born."[10]

Knowing when and how to talk about yourself is as important a skill as listening. No one really gets close to the kind of person who's so careful about her image she never reveals anything intimate. You've got to open up, but not too wide. In other words, if you reveal too much you'll overwhelm the other person. Nobody appreciates a babbler mouth who unloads unedited memories that could interest only a mother. And one more caution about self-disclosing: don't replace it with gossip and think you'll accomplish the same thing. Everyone warms to the person who tells tales on him or herself. But there's nothing more repellent than the person who's constantly telling you some horrible secret about someone else.

> *A friend to all is a friend to none.*
> —*English Proverb*

●◆ *Exercise 14: Are You a "Growth Promoting" Listener?*

Everyone knows how to listen, right? Wrong. This exercise in the *Relationships Workbook* will help you determine what kind of listener you are and help you hone your listening skills.

HOW WE KEEP TRUE FRIENDS

It's one thing to start a friendship, it's quite another to maintain it, to stay on what Lewis called "the same secret path." Even strong friendships require watering or they shrivel up and blow away. That's why George Bernard Shaw touched an exposed nerve in both of us when we read the words he scribbled to his friend Archibald Henderson: "I have neglected you shockingly of late. This is because I have had to neglect everything that could be neglected without immediate ruin, and partly because you have passed into the circle of intimate friends whose feelings one never dreams of considering."

It's so easy to take good friends for granted. And in a sense, we should. Like a comfortable pair of gloves, old friends wear well. But friendships that suffer from busyness and overfamiliarity can't afford to be neglected too long. They need renewal. And to suggest that there are techniques for maintaining authentic relationships would be to devalue the dignity friendship deserves. Such a meaningful relationship cannot be reduced to "easy steps." Research has revealed, however, the qualities that keep true friendship alive and well. So we offer a list of the most important qualities for your contemplation. Like Shaw, you may neglect your intimate friends from time to time, but if you fail to cultivate these qualities—loyalty, forgiveness, honesty, and dedication—you can't expect to keep true friends.

Loyalty

The quality that tops the list in survey after survey of what people appreciate most about their friends is loyalty. It seems nothing, but *nothing*, matters more than being true. Good friends keep their promises. They don't tell your secrets to other people. And they don't desert you, even when you are in trouble.

Harry Truman's secretary of state, Dean Acheson, caused quite a stir when he visited his friend Alger Hiss in prison. Hiss was a convicted traitor, and it was bad politics to have any association with him. But when prudent politicians condemned Acheson publicly, Acheson simply said, "A friend does not forsake a friend just because he is in jail." That's loyalty.

The famous maxim that "a friend in need is a friend indeed" is not the entire story of loyalty, however. A friend in triumph may be even harder to find. Isn't it easier to be a savior than a cheerleader for our friends? It takes twenty-four-karat loyalty for a friend to soar alongside us when we are flying high rather than to bring us down to earth. Loyal friends not only lend a hand when you're in need; they applaud your successes and cheer you on without envy when you prosper.

━━━

●◆ *Exercise 15: Are You a Fair-weather Friend?*

Since loyalty is so central to building a good friendship, it deserves some serious attention. It also deserves some self-reflection and assessment. This exercise in the *Relationships Workbook* will help you explore how loyal you tend to be to your friends.

━━━

Forgiveness

As important as loyalty is, our friendships don't always have it. Enter forgiveness. Every friend you'll ever have will eventually disappoint you. Count on it. That doesn't mean that every offense of a friend requires forgiveness; some slights need only be overlooked and forgotten. Winston Churchill's mother, Jennie, understood this when she said, "Treat your friends as you do your pictures, and place them in their best light."

Too many good relationships fade because some slight—real or imagined—cancels it out. Some people pout, brood, or blow up if their friend is not speedy enough in returning a phone call or if they are not included in a social event. They set such high standards for the relationship that they're constantly being disappointed. They can't let little things go; every minor lapse becomes a betrayal.

Real betrayal, the kind that leaves you hanging out to dry, is another matter altogether, and we'll get to that in the next chapter. At issue here is the idea of overlooking and, yes, sometimes forgiving the occasional pain that comes with friendship.

By the way, forgiveness is a two-way street. Unless you are a saint, you are bound to offend—intentionally or unintentionally—every friend deeply at least once in the course of time, and if the relationship survives it will be because your friend forgives. The friends we keep the longest are the friends who forgave us the most. And the essence of true friendship is knowing what to overlook.

Honesty

"Les, you can be so focused on achieving a goal," a friend of mine recently told me, "that you sometimes lose sight of other people's opinions and feelings in the process." Ouch. That stung. But Steve was right. We were having lunch at our favorite coffee shop when he lowered the boom. Actually, Steve was looking out for my best interest. He cares about me and didn't want me to get into a sticky situation with the members of a committee I was chairing. And it's a good thing. His honesty saved my neck.

> Do not use a hatchet to remove a fly from your friend's forehead.
> — Chinese Proverb

True friends are like that. Honesty is a prerequisite to their relationship. "Genuine friendship cannot exist where one of the parties is unwilling to hear the truth," says Cicero, "and the other is equally indisposed to speak it."[11] Does this require brutal honesty? Not exactly. It requires honesty that is carefully dealt in the context of respect. In the absence of respect, you see, honesty is a lethal weapon. Perhaps that's what caused Cicero to add, "Remove respect from friendship and you have taken away the most splendid ornament it possesses."

Honesty is not only expressed in words; it means being authentic. I have known people who become fast friends because they have so much in common. Their work, their wardrobes, their tastes, their background are all in sync. They become like twins who can finish each other's thoughts, not to mention sentences. But the relationship is not real. One or both of them is so eager to have a kindred spirit that they become someone they aren't just to get along. And the relationship becomes what Emerson called "a mush of concession."

True friends aren't afraid to be honest and they aren't afraid to be themselves. True friends follow Emerson's advice: "Better be a nettle in the side of your friend than his echo." Translation: If you are afraid of making enemies, you'll never have true friends.

Dedication

It was 12:30 in the morning. We had just returned to our room after speaking to a group of students at a retreat center in the backwoods of Kentucky. A loud knocking broke the silence. "Who could that be?" I wondered.

Leslie opened the door. "Monty Lobb!" she exclaimed. We couldn't believe it. Our good college buddy living in Cincinnati had driven four hours—one way—and tracked us down without directions or an address.

"I knew I could find you," he said with a big bear hug. "I heard you were near Wilmore, and I just had to see you." He brought a boxed chocolate cake and a couple of plastic forks he'd picked up on his long drive. So we ate cake while we talked and laughed for about an hour and a half. Monty then had to leave. He was teaching Sunday school that morning at his church back in Cincinnati—another four hours on the road.

Few acts of friendship have spoken more loudly about personal dedication to us than what Monty did for our relationship. The bottom line? He made time. No, he *sacrificed* time to be with us. That's the meaning of dedication. It refers to the ability of two people to influence each other's

> In each of my friends there is some-
> thing that only some other friend can
> fully bring out. By myself I am not
> large enough to call the whole person
> into activity; I want other lights than
> my own to show all his facets. Hence
> true friendship is the least jealous of
> loves.
>
> —C. S. Lewis

plans, thoughts, actions, and emotions.

Think about it. Back when you were a kid, the hours spent with friends were too numerous to count. Contemporary life, with its tight schedules and crowded appointment books, however, has forced most friendships into something requiring a good deal of intentionality and pursuit just to keep them going. Post-college friendships require setting aside an evening during which to squeeze in all your news and advice, confession and opinion. This intimate compress of information occurs only through dedication.

Of course, dedication becomes most salient in times of crisis. When a friend's emotional bottoming out, for example, means canceling a date to provide a shoulder of support. That's what friends are for. So don't complain about having fair-weather friends if you are unwilling to be inconvenienced.

Personal sacrifice. Selfless devotion. Commitment. These are the noble qualities dedication requires.

➪ Exercise 16: Determining Your Dedication Quotient

When it comes to maintaining and renewing your friendships, loyalty, forgiveness, and honesty are critical. This exercise in the *Relationships Workbook*, however, focuses on dedication. It will ask you if you have it and if not, it will show you how to get it.

FOR REFLECTION

• It has been said that many people audition to be our friends, but only a few make the cut. What is it about your friends that caused them to get the part? Did it have more to do with circumstances or personal qualities?

- The medical benefits of having friends is quite remarkable. What benefits of the less scientific kind do you appreciate? What fruits of friendship do you enjoy the most?

- Do you agree that generally speaking, our good friends come in two forms: as friends of the road and friends of the heart? Think of an example of a meaningful friendship that did not last. What purpose did it serve in your life or what passage did it see you through?

- Forgiveness can be one of the most challenging struggles for any relationship. Think of a time when you were either on the receiving or the giving end of forgiveness. What makes it so difficult?

- Of the four qualities that keep friendships going—loyalty, forgiveness, honesty, and dedication—which one is most important to you and why? What other qualities would you add to this list?

chapter five

What to Do
When Friends Fail

From strong relationships often comes great grief.
—⚡ Irish Proverb

When the phone rang in the middle of the night I (Les) never expected it to be Danny. "I'm calling from France," he said. "I know this is crazy but I needed to talk to you."

As I was still rubbing the sleep from my eyes he told me that he had been thinking about our friendship—make that our ex-friendship. "I don't know exactly what happened between us," he confessed, "but I do know I acted like a jerk and I wanted to apologize." He was sincere, and his heartfelt apology caught me off guard. I didn't expect to ever hear from Danny again, let alone hear him apologize.

It had been three years since we were in school together—three years since our last strained, polite conversation where we both knew the gulf between us had grown too wide to cross.

On the phone that night, however, Danny was attempting to build a bridge, if only temporary, to reconnect and make things right. He told me about a soul-searching experience he was going through and how he didn't want to carry any resentment or bitterness over our failed friendship.

We both apologized for past insensitivities and laughed at how comical it all seemed in retrospect. It was a cleansing. A wrong had been righted, a lost friend found. We still aren't that close, geographically or emotionally, but we have a connection. And in a sense we're quite lucky—most friendships that fade are gone forever. Very few are strong enough to make us wish for a second chance.

There are times when all of us look closely at a friendship and realize that it just isn't working. It may be a fairly new friendship that still has a few wrinkles in it, or it may be a longtime friendship that was once rock solid but now appears to be fracturing. Either way, when a friendship falters we are rarely equipped for the aftershock.

Close friends, after all, often become like siblings—some "closer than a brother." But losing a close friend is not at all like losing a family member. We tend not to grieve the loss of a friend; there is no memorial service for a shattered friendship. Most people don't have screaming blowouts or this-is-the-end discussions or final, definite breaks. They don't seek shoulders to cry on to grieve the loss of friends like they do the loss of a family member or a romantic relationship. They don't go to counselors either to heal the relationship or to cope with the loss. Indeed, despite the apparent premium so many people put on making friends, there is a surprising lack of focus in popular culture on the processes and feelings at work when friendships end. There are no best-sellers or self-help guides, and except for the rather vague and undescriptive term "a falling out," there's not even much of a vocabulary to describe what happens, let alone why.

> Friendships, in general, are suddenly contracted; and therefore it is no wonder they are easily dissolved.
>
> —Joseph Addison

This chapter is an attempt to change all that. Here you will learn not only *why* but *how* friends sometimes fail. We'll take a hard look at irreconcilable differences (both real and imagined) and give you practical tools for determining whether a sinking friendship has any chance of staying afloat. We'll show you how to repair a broken friendship or grieve its loss if need be. We begin, however, by pondering a critically important question, one that will set the stage for the rest of this chapter.

HOW MUCH CAN YOU EXPECT FROM A FRIEND?

Why start with this question? Because your answer is a pretty good barometer of how well your friendships will weather relational storms. Let's face it, we don't ask much of casual friendships, the kind in which you invite each other to a party once a year. But we demand more than you might guess from friendships characterized by strong feelings and a shared history. We expect friendships to be easier, more automatic than they actually are.

Think about your childhood friendships. They often set the tone for all the rest. You never "worked" on first-grade friendships, they just happened. Andy, my first "best friend," for example, lived just two houses down from me, and we literally met in the sandbox at school. The bond was almost instant. He liked Hot Wheels and Tonka trucks. So did I. What's to discuss? It was the beginning of a beautiful friendship—until his family moved to Texas that next summer.

> The most fatal disease of friendship is gradual decay, or dislike hourly increased by causes too slender for complaint, and too numerous for removal.
>
> —Samuel Johnson

Andy's departure pretty much marked the end of trouble-free friendships in my life. Just a few short years later, sandbox bliss was replaced by the tormented, possessive feelings of a third-grade relationship where blatant betrayal reared its head. That's when I learned that my new best friend, Donny, was playing at another classmate's house after school. Sound familiar? It happens to nearly all of us.

There may be worse betrayals in store, but probably none is more influential than the sudden fickleness of an elementary-school friend who has dropped us for someone more popular after all our careful, patient wooing. *It shouldn't be that way,* we think to ourselves. But alas it is. It's the lesson our friendships continually teach us, a lesson we don't want to learn: *Friendships are fragile.*

The seeming ease of friendships—compared to romantic and family relationships (more likely loaded with emotional baggage)—is part of the reason we value friendships so much. Relatively speaking, friendships just happen. Which makes it all the harder to accept the fact that these "easy" relationships are not a terribly resilient bond.

Most of us are surprised, even resentful, when once-effortless friendships turn rocky.[1] During the honeymoon period of friendship, which usually lasts anywhere from a few months to more than a year, each friend puts his or her best foot forward. Honeymooning friends tend to overlook irritating habits and may not even be aware of major character flaws or value differences. So when they emerge, we feel betrayed.

What's worse, we like to think of close friends as mirror images of ourselves. And if a friend isn't quite as perfect as we'd originally thought—and hardly anyone is—he or she can be seen as a bad reflection on us. Getting beyond this feeling requires an acceptance of separateness and uniqueness. It requires an honest answer to the question: How much can you expect from your friends? And if your answer is nothing short of perfection, you'll need to brace yourself for a bumpy ride. To be honest, however, even if your expectations are lower, the road is rarely found without unexpected potholes. It's enough to leave even the most stalwart asking why.

Exercise 17: What You Expect from Friends

Each of us comes to our friendships with a slightly different set of expectations. This exercise in the *Relationships Workbook* will help you assess your expectations so you will be better equipped to determine if and how your expectations need adjusting.

WHY FRIENDS FAIL

One day, after a string of unsatisfactory phone calls or after a few strained talks at a coffee shop or maybe an all-out blowout, you mutter to yourself, "What am I doing? Why am I talking to this person? He no longer feels like a friend, but I don't know why." *Why?* we ask.

Why would a once sturdy and fulfilling friendship suddenly, or even gradually, falter?

The answer is actually rather straightforward. Most

> Most people enjoy the inferiority of their best friends.
>
> — Lord Chesterfield

friendships break for one of three main reasons: a major change such as marriage or a move; neglect; or the betrayal of a confidence. In an attempt to better prepare ourselves for these almost inevitable occurrences, we'll take a closer look at each one.

Change

Perhaps the most frequent source of friendship turmoil is the disruption resulting from a major change—for better or worse—in the life of a friend. When one friend's dream is realized before the other's, for example, the two get out of sync, and jealousy, anger, or pity can take over. Even well-established friendships can be thrown out of kilter by a major job promotion, the beginning of a serious romantic relationship, and above all, marriage. The change factor is part emotional and part practical. Since most friendships begin when both people are going through similar experiences, when something big happens to change the status of one friend, it's human nature for the other to feel some envy—"Why her and not me?" During periods of change, the discovery of new limits on time, energy, and attention is often the real source of contention between friends. The friend whose life has changed least will usually have to make more accommodations, at least during the initial period of transition. Whatever the case, you can count on change to impact even your most treasured lifelong friendships.

Neglect

There is a line in Woody Allen's film *Annie Hall* where he says to Diane Keaton: "A relationship, I think, is like a shark, you know? It has to constantly move forward or it dies. And I think what we got on our hands is a dead shark." Some friendships die because they aren't moving forward. They die from stagnation or plain old neglect. You meant to call but didn't. You knew it was his birthday, but were too busy to celebrate (he'd understand). But friendships *need* to be nurtured. It's as simple as that. Without nurturance, annoyance is sure to set in.

Think about it. When we're busy, we only do what comes easy, and even good friendships aren't always easy. So if your friend has an annoying trait, if she's loud, or cheap, or a habitual complainer, you are more likely to neglect the relationship. Of course the same is true in the opposite direction when your friend is neglecting *you*. Whether it's you or her, however, neglect is sure to cause a rift. And when it does, it almost always catches us off guard, when we least expect it or can least handle it: when we're going through stressful times at school, work, or home that make us less attentive and less able to respond—which is what caused the neglect to begin with. That's why it can seem that the best friendships break precisely when we need them the most.

Betrayal

She's your best pal, and you tell her everything—only to find out that she's gossiped about you or, even worse, flirted with your boyfriend. When a once-trusted confidant double-crosses you, betrayal is the result. And while change and neglect may be more common reasons for failed friendships, betrayal is almost always more painful. Why? Because betrayal dismantles trust.

> It is more shameful to distrust one's friends than to be deceived by them.
>
> —François, Duc de La Rochefoucauld

Your confidant, who knows your darkest secrets (how deeply you're in debt or your struggle with an eating disorder, for example), has let one of them out of the bag. After all, your close friend has the power to hurt you precisely because she knows you so well; your deepest secrets provide her with the emotional ammunition that can cut you to the core. And you're left wondering if she will do it again.

Maybe your friend, whom you counted on, isn't there for you in a time of need. Or perhaps she joins others in teasing you about a sensitive issue. Which brings up an important point: What we perceive as betrayal is often unintentional; your friend may not think what she did was wrong or realize that she's caused you pain. She may not have known you were counting on her so much. She may have thought you found her teasing funny, not hurtful. If your friend is acting out of anger or jealousy, however, and is thus seeking revenge, look out. You are now the victim of blatant betrayal. Whether intentional or not, betrayal is a guaranteed toxin to every friendship.

Whether you find yourself in the midst of a friendship failure that is the result of change, neglect, or betrayal, the steps to rebuilding it— if, indeed, that is what needs to be done—are quite similar. Before exploring these steps, however, we pose an important preliminary question: Are the differences between you and your friend truly irreconcilable, and if so, what's the best way to call it quits?

➰ Exercise 18: Learning from Your Own Failed Friendships

If we do not learn from failure, we are passing up a valuable form of education. By taking a fresh look at how some of our relationships did not work out, we can learn much to improve our current and our new ones. This exercise in the *Relationships Workbook* will help you do just that.

IRRECONCILABLE DIFFERENCES?

Friendships die with a bang or whimper. Those that whimper simply dissolve from neglect, having run their natural course. They quietly cross some threshold, and the break comes to pass without much fanfare. It is normal, even appropriate, to shed friends throughout our lives: when we leave school, when we change jobs, when we move to a new city, even when we drop an aerobics class. Start a new romance, get married, have children, and you probably leave behind a wake of friends.

Friendships ending with a bang are more likely the result of an unexpected change or a more dreadful betrayal. You amass enough

> Woe to him who is alone when he falls
> and has not another to lift him up.
>
> —⁑ Ecclesiastes 4:10 RSV

incremental bitterness (or it comes in one lump sum) and you have one too many unsatisfying encounters, then one of you erupts. You come to the end of your journey together, say good riddance, and take different paths.

Regardless of how a friendship breaks, with a bang or a whimper, you will inevitably find yourself wondering whether it should be repaired, whether you should do what you can to salvage what is left or just let it go. That's a good question, by the way, because not every friendship should be saved. Sometimes the cost is just too high. But there's no hard-and-fast rule; each of us has to decide what is and isn't fundamentally important to us.

If you value a relationship that has come to the end of the road, we urge you not to write it off completely—at least not just yet. Okay, so you've been burned, betrayed in a way you never deserved. You want to get even. But you have a choice: you can experience some momentary satisfaction by slamming the door shut and keeping it locked with resentment, or you can give yourself space and time to cool off and collect your thoughts. The point is that if you cherish a friendship you shouldn't be too quick to burn all of your bridges—even if you're far apart at the moment. It may be a cliché, but time really does have a way of healing deep hurts. Time allows forgiveness to wash away anger and keep us healthy.

Since we're tossing around clichés, allow us to remind you of another: "A friend in need is a friend indeed." What this means is that when life deals you a bitter hand it will be your old friends you seek out. When a tragedy happens—a career setback or the loss of a parent, for example—you realize life is too short to hold on to grudges. Tragedy reminds us what is really important in life—our relationships. It can spur us on to rebuild bridges once burned in anger. Talking with an old friend, after all, can remind us that life was not always so bleak, and it can give us hope that our world will regain its equilibrium. So do what you can to leave the door open.

But let's be honest. Sometimes we simply cannot repair a friendship, even though we've tried and tried and tried. Sometimes, no matter how terribly sad it makes us, we have to accept the fact that a friendship has died. After all, no friendship can weather a crisis if only one person wants to preserve the relationship. When that's the case, the best we can do is grieve the loss. We must note those things we will miss because that person is no longer a central part in our life and accept the fact that the relationship is over. We must give ourselves permission to feel sad. And we must move on.

Many broken friendships are destined to stay that way. Renewals are mostly reserved for those special, intimate friendships, the ones that brought meaning to our lives. Even then it can often seem impossible to fit the pieces back together. But there are good reasons to try: the restored relationship can give us perspective on our experiences, deepen our lives. The stronger for being broken, such a friendship can help us carry on our lives with greater satisfaction. The remainder of this chapter is dedicated to helping you restore your broken relationships.

➡ Exercise 19: Can This Friendship Be Saved?

Not every failed friendship is meant to be revived. This exercise in the *Relationships Workbook* will help you pinpoint specific signs in your relationship to help you determine whether or not it shows promising signs of survival.

MENDING BROKEN FRIENDSHIPS

When two people forge a friendship, invest a lot of time and energy in its development, then bitterly break apart, that doesn't necessarily mean the relationship is gone forever. Not all friendship fissures are fatal.

If you have a long-lost friend with whom things ended badly, you may be able to make a meaningful reconnection. The following five-step plan will help you determine whether or not a particular friendship should be saved and, if so, how you can do it. While these specific steps should not be treated as *the* answer for reconciling every failed friendship, they can serve as general principles for guiding you in your unique journey.

Step One: Count the Cost

You must determine whether your fractured friendship should be repaired. An unhealthy relationship is not worth repairing if it forces you to compromise your principles or subvert your self-respect. You have the right to ask a friend to change if he or she is making you feel less cared about, less respected, or even worried. If your friend is pressuring you into something you want no part of, for example, and you stand by your convictions, a good friend will understand and respect that. He or she may even change as a result. If not, you're probably better off without such a destructive relationship.

> Friendship is like money, easier made than kept.
>
> — Samuel Butler

Realizing that a friendship no longer works can be a positive step. "I spent more than a year wondering why I didn't feel terrific about one of my friends who seemed very affectionate," someone recently told us in a counseling session. "Eventually I realized that she was competing with me. So I decided to pull away. We still talk from time to time, but we're no longer tight, and the relationship no longer drains me."

If you find yourself knowing that a friendship is unhealthy for you but you keep pursuing it, we urge you to assess your relational neediness. Don't fall into the trap of believing that if you lose a friend you'll never find another. The opposite may be true: you may not make another friend until you sever your association with an unhealthy person.[2] The point is that just as good friendships can boost your sense of belonging, bad friendships can undermine your security and self-worth.

So carefully consider the price you pay for keeping a faltering friendship alive. And if the cost is too high, make a clean break. Don't

drift away or behave badly. Not taking phone calls or canceling dates—
even when justified—can block the lessons to be learned from the
unworkable friendship. If you seek closure in a more direct and responsible way by exploring your feelings together, it is likely to pay off (for
both of you) in greater openness in your new friendships.

If, on the other hand, your friendship is worth the cost of repairing and maintaining it—if it has redeeming qualities you value—you're
ready for the next step.

Step Two: Make Meaningful Contact

If you have decided it's wise to reestablish contact, you need to
write a note or call the person to convey one primary message: "Our
friendship is valuable to me, and I miss seeing you. Is there any way
we can resolve what stands between us?" That's all. In making contact
the point is simple, to convey your desire and explore their openness
to considering a discussion. At this stage, there is no need to go into airing your grievances or even making elaborate apologies (that will come
later). For now, you are simply calling a peace talk to open up honest
discussions about bringing resolution to your relationship.

This step, though it appears quite simple and straightforward, is
where things often get dicey. You will unknowingly sabotage your simple message if you are not aware of any lingering desires to get even with
this person. And it is impossible to be humble and make meaningful
contact in a genuine way if you are hanging on to anger and resentment.
There is a key to releasing these toxic emotions, however, and it is found
in the next step.

Step Three: Forgive as Best You Can

I've always found it difficult to bury the proverbial hatchet. If I've
been wronged, it's tough enough to let it go even after the person says
"I'm sorry." But to take the initiative in forgiving is down right impossible. At least it seems so. Who wants to turn the other cheek? Isn't that

the act of a coward or even a fool? It's always seemed so to me; that is, until I learned a valuable secret.

When someone slights you, offends you, or deeply hurts you, the urge to respond in kind is natural: an eye for an eye, a tooth for a tooth. The problem with this urge is that we don't know when to stop. If we lose an eye, we want more than an eye in return. Truth be known, we don't want to balance the scales, we want them tipped in our favor (our legal system attests to this fact). And once we feel the compensation is satisfactory, our enemy takes his turn at punishing us again. The cycle repeats itself over and over.

Forgiveness puts an end to all that. Our primal urge for "balancing the score" comes to a screeching halt when we set our pride aside and begin to forgive. It's for our own advantage. Why? Because getting even takes its toll not only on the offender, but on the one seeking revenge as well. When Jesus tells us to "turn the other cheek" or "go the extra mile," he is not telling us to give our enemy some advantage over us. He is not telling us to be cowards. Cheek-turning is for our own protection. Once you free yourself from a desire to hurt back, you put an end to your vindictive spirit and save yourself from further harm.

But let's get real. How do we do this? How do we forgive? It begins by setting our pride aside and trying our best to see the situation from the other person's perspective. In fact, if you are not open to seeing the other side of the story, you will never be able to approach your friend in a meaningful way. If you think the problems that are cooling down your friendship are totally and completely the fault of your friend, think again. The problems that plague a friendship are rarely one hundred percent the other person's fault. If you keep this in mind you will be well on your way to practicing forgiveness instead of trying to balance the scales.

And remember, the truth is we can never balance the scales. "Do not repay anyone evil for evil," says the apostle Paul, instead "live at peace."[3] That's the result of forgiveness: peace. Sweet peace. And it sets the tone for the next step in repairing your friendship.

Step Four: Diagnose the Problem

I (Les) had an amazing conversation recently with a guy who was feeling terribly lonely. I asked a standard question: "Do you have any close friends?"

"Nope. I'm friendly with people at work but I'm not close with anyone."

"Why not?" I asked.

"Well, a few years ago I

> Often we have no time for our friends but all the time in the world for our enemies.
> —Leon Uris

was real friendly with this guy. We used to work out together several times a week. Then one week he didn't show up. I heard from a mutual acquaintance at work that he was upset over something I said. That was the last time I ever saw him."

His story confused me. "What was it that offended him?" I asked.

"I have no idea."

I was incredulous. "You mean you never asked him what happened?"

"Nope, I just dropped it there. I decided that if he was going to get upset like that, what's the use?"

What a sad story. Here is a guy who had a good friend, yet because of a minor misunderstanding, the friendship disintegrated. What baffled me is that *he had not taken the trouble to find out what had gone wrong.*

This scenario is more common than you think, especially in the process of trying to rebuild a connection. But finding out what went wrong is critically important if we are to learn what caused the problem in the first place—and avoid repeating it.

One of the reasons we avoid diagnosing the problem is that we don't like to acknowledge that there *is* a problem. We know that "everybody's human," but we often assign larger-than-life qualities to certain individuals, and if they are a "good friend" we see them as all good, but when they let us down we tend to see them as all bad. We want people to be neater than they are, less complicated. We don't want to face the fact that people are partially good and partially bad. Viewing things in black and white seems easier and more practical. But most of life, including our friendships, comes in shades of gray. And if you don't accept that, you miss out on a lot of relationships that might have been. So don't pretend there's no problem. Diagnose it together and move to the next step. After all, if a friendship can't survive an honest discussion of differences, that may be a sign that the relationship ought to end.

Step Five: Rebuild Respect

Roman statesman and philosopher Cicero, who wrote perhaps the best treatise ever on friendship, insisted that what brings true friends together is "a mutual belief in each other's goodness." This insistence on virtue as a precondition for true friendship may seem difficult to cultivate when a friend has let you down, but it is essential. That's why the final step in mending a broken relationship is rebuilding respect for your friend. Most likely, your respect for him or her has been battered and bruised, so it will take some nurturing. But if your friendship is to survive it will ultimately depend on the reviving of respect. "Remove respect from friendship," said Cicero, "and you have taken away the most splendid ornament it possesses."

You may be wondering just how one revives respect for a fallen friend.

We suggest two things. You begin by noting your friend's most admirable qualities. Ask yourself, what traits does he or she possess that inspire you to become a better person? Make a list of these qualities of character. If you're like most people, you may find yourself weighing these good qualities against the bad. That's okay. The point is not to whitewash your friend's personality. In fact, you may discover that he or she is simply deficient as a certain kind of friend. Some friends, for example, are great when you need a ride to pick up your car from the shop, but no help at all when you're in despair over a lost love. Once you know a friendship's limits, it's easier to enjoy it for what it is without feeling let down about what it's not. The goal here is rebuild your

respect by highlighting those
qualities you like best about
your friend.

Next, you need to own up
to your end of the relationship
by offering a sincere apology
for not being the kind of friend you could have been. Identify specific
things you did that contributed to the friendship's failure and confess
them to your friend in an apology. Take ownership and ask for forgiveness. Above all, remember that an apology is only as good as the
spirit behind it. "A true apology is more than just acknowledgment of
a mistake," Norman Vincent Peale once said. "It is recognition that
something you have said or done has damaged a relationship and that
you care enough about the relationship to want it repaired and
restored." If you do that, mutual respect is almost certain.

> *Laughter is not at all a bad beginning for a friendship, and it is far the best ending for one.*
>
> *—Oscar Wilde*

•◊ Exercise 20: Making Amends

Knowing what to do and actually doing it are two different things. Even if we understand what to do, we all need
a little help in putting that knowledge to work. This exercise in the *Relationships Workbook* will help you apply the five-
step plan for mending a broken relationship to a specific
friendship in your own life.

IS THE GAIN WORTH THE PAIN?

Perhaps you are still wondering whether all the work involved in
repairing a broken relationship is worth it. Unfortunately we can't guarantee that it is. Some relationships, no matter how hard you try, never
recover the joy they once had. But if you feel a pang of regret or remorse
when you think about a former friend and do nothing about it, you'll
never know what might have been. And even if the relationship isn't
revived, you'll never know the satisfaction that comes from trying.

That was what I (Leslie) learned in an attempt to recover my lost
relationship with Renee. When we first met, Renee and I had lots in

common. As part-time coworkers on the same office staff, we shared an almost instant camaraderie. We were also part-time graduate students while our new husbands were enrolled full-time in the same rigorous doctoral program. We confided in one another. We commiserated about school bills and stress. We depended on each other for prayer support as well as honest feedback. And we always made each other laugh.

That all changed, however, after graduation when Les and I announced our plans to move to Seattle. At first, Renee shared my excitement about the transition and even orchestrated an elaborate and personal celebration in the form of a going-away party. She gave me a gold engraved bracelet that day to remind me of our friendship. When Les and I moved from Pasadena, I was convinced that my friendship with Renee would last a lifetime. But it didn't.

Almost immediately Renee seemed distant, not only geographically, but emotionally. Our phone conversations turned almost icy. I told myself it was just an adjustment period that would improve. But it didn't. When I gently confronted Renee with my feelings, it only seemed to add to the agonizing awkwardness. With the exception of an occasional Christmas card, contact between us virtually stopped. A friendship I considered to be of priceless value mysteriously vanished.

Four years later, I phoned Renee, not necessarily to rebuild our friendship but to bring a bit of closure to what happened between us. "I know you didn't expect to hear from me," I told her, "but I just wanted you to know I still think about our days in Pasadena with fondness and wanted to see how you were doing." Renee sounded like her old self: warm, enthusiastic, and funny. What surprised me, however, was Renee's confession of remorse about our lost connection. Renee told me that saying good-bye to me stirred up a storm of personal issues in her own life about loss and betrayal and that our relationship suffered the consequences. We caught up on each other's lives for a while and then said good-bye once more, knowing we would never fully bridge the gulf that time and space had brought between us.

That day on the phone was bittersweet. It was marked with relief as well as regret. Both of us knew there would be no going back to the way things once were. This was a friendship reconciled, but not recovered. Was that enough? Was it worth the effort? You bet. We still exchange Christmas cards and the occasional letter—more in tribute to the friendship we once shared than as an expression of our current connection.

In their own way, even failed friendships last.

FOR REFLECTION

- As you consider particular friendships you have lost along the way, are there some that are more important to you than others? If so, why? What makes them valuable to you, and how do you feel about rebuilding a connection with them?
- What do you think about the idea that what we expect from our friendships will determine whether or not those friendships can hold up under turbulent times? Think of some examples of expectations of a friend that cross the line. How do you determine that?
- The chapter points out that most friendships fail because of one of three things: positive or negative change in one person's life, neglect of the relationship, or blatant betrayal that is either intentional or unintentional. As you consider your own failed friendships, what can the cause tell you about finding a "cure"?
- How can you, personally, determine whether a broken relationship should be repaired or not? In other words, how do you decide if your differences are truly irreconcilable or not?
- When it comes to the practical side of mending a broken relationship with a friend, which of the five steps suggested in this chapter (count the cost, make contact, forgive, diagnose the problem, and rebuild respect) would be most difficult for you to take and why? What could you do to make taking this step a bit easier?

chapter six

Falling in Love
Without
Losing Your Mind

Love is possible only if two persons communicate with each other from the center of their existence.

—⌐ Erich Fromm

She shifted her posture. Her head tilted slightly, her shoulders lifted, and she gently fluffed her auburn hair. Suddenly, our eyes locked for a moment. She smiled, then slowly dropped her eyelids; tilted her head down and to the side. I felt dizzy and faint, as if my legs had turned to warm lead. But I wasn't about to let this signal go unanswered. If I was reading her body language correctly—and I was—she was giving me the universal signal to approach. I did.

Without saying a word I walked toward her and reached for her hand. Every nerve ending in my fingers carried a rush of excitement to my brain. We looked at each other, only for a moment, but I could have described every contour of her face.

"Has everyone found a partner?" the voice over the loudspeaker asked. Then, suddenly, through the same crackling sound system, the piano pounded, the fiddle jumped, and the pulse pushed through the gymnasium as a latent charge of prepubescent neurochemicals enveloped the building. From there on the caller's cues determined our actions. Along with thirty other awkward sixth-grade couples we kicked back from each other, then pulled together again. For eight long beats, we stared into each other's eyes. All else faded into the background. You guessed it. We were in gym class learning to square dance ... and I was in love.

Her name was Caroline O'Toole, if I'm not mistaken. We never spoke a word to each other, and I can't tell you a thing about her life now. But I still remember the feelings I had that day in the gym. This girl, I thought (or should I say I felt), was the one for me. My feelings were too magical, too strong to mean anything else.

Not much changes as we mature. Love, it seems, is ruled by over-powering, unexplainable, mystical emotions. The ancient Greeks compared falling in love to going insane. So have modern writers. "It is the taking over of a rational and lucid mind by delusion and self-destruction," writes American author Marilyn French. "You lose yourself, you have no power over yourself, you can't even think straight."[1] Researchers have verified these hunches about the dizzying effect of falling in love. Michael Liebowitz of New York State Psychiatric Institute has shown that when a passionate attraction occurs, a chemical substance (called phenylethylamine) is released in the brain, causing feelings of elation and excitement, along with physical sensations such as light-headedness and a sense of being short of breath.

Even before there were scientific experiments, poets and philosophers had long noted the psychological effects of love. As Nietzsche put it: "Love is the state in which man sees things most widely different from what they are. The force of illusion reaches its zenith here." Shakespeare put it this way: "Love is blind, and lovers cannot see the pretty follies that themselves commit." And William Blake had his say on the subject as well: "Love ... breaks all chains from every mind."

Indeed, steamy starts do not promote our best thinking. Intense emotions often block us from taking a careful and objective look at ourselves, the person we are dating, and the relationship we are forming together.[2] Falling in love tells us nothing about whether a relationship

is healthy or good for us. Intense feelings of love, no matter how consuming, are hardly
a measure of true and enduring
closeness. But tell that to our
feelings.

> To say the truth, reason and love keep
> little company together now-a-days.
> —William Shakespeare

Too many people lose their mind when they fall in love. And that's
when the real insanity—and eventual heartache—begins. This chapter provides an alternative. We call it smart love. And it will help you
evaluate your romantic relationships with your head, not just your heart.
We begin by defining exactly what smart love is and devote the bulk
of the chapter to showing you how it works. We conclude with a brief
discussion on keeping your love life sane once you've found somebody
to love.

One more thing before we begin. If you think it's somehow less
exhilarating or romantic to fall in love with your brain turned on, ask
yourself this: Would you bungee jump without the cord? Of course not.
And if your love life is void of critical capacities, you're headed for certain disaster. This chapter will help you keep your critical capacities
intact and the thrill alive.

WHAT'S YOUR LOVE I.Q.?

Imagine walking into a crowded room, briefly milling around, and
then with the help of a little computer technology, knowing, without
ever saying a word, whether anyone there might be a good match for
you as a dating partner. Sound like sci-fi? Not to researchers at M.I.T.'s
Media Lab who designed Thinking Tags.[3] These little wearable com-
puters seek out other "smart" tags in a room and swap data. The
microchip-driven, infrared-transmitting cards are programmable by the
wearer, who is asked to input responses to five questions designed to
help you click with another. At a Thinking Tag get-together, people
wander about and let their badges do the work. When they approach
within five feet of each other, pairs of tags display their results in a neat

row of five red and green lights. According to the inventors, you dispense with all the tired chitchat and immediately know whether it's worth the brain cycles to attempt social intercourse.

> The affections are like lightening: you cannot tell where they will strike till they have fallen.
>
> —Jean Baptiste Lacordaire

If this artificial-intelligence approach to interaction seems a bit, well, artificial, we understand. Thinking Tags, as far as we know, are far from catching on. When it comes to getting to know one another, most people still opt for old-fashioned communication (even if it's on the Internet). But you don't have to sacrifice relational intelligence if you're not wearing a smart tag. Not if you have what we call a high Love I.Q.

Have you ever thought about your intelligence when it comes to love? Not your understanding of its history or origins. But your capacity to keep your wits about you when you're engulfed by its mysterious emotions. That's what smart love is all about. It doesn't take the fun out of feeling. Smart love is still love, thrills and all, only wiser. More focused. More observant. Smart love doesn't allow you to delude yourself into believing something that isn't true. It may, for example, point out that the person you're with is the person you're better off without. On the other hand, it may help you see clearly that the person you're with makes you a better person. It may give you confidence to know that your relationship is headed in the right direction.

While your heart is sweetly distracted by all the possibilities, smart love keeps you aware of what is taking place. You still swoon and sigh, but you also consider facts and make intelligent choices. Smart love is all about falling in love without losing your mind.

➥ Exercise 21: What's Your Love I.Q.?

Have your ever considered how "love smart" you are? If left to your own devices, would you make wise romantic relationship choices? This exercise in the *Relationships Workbook* will help you determine your natural aptitude and acumen when it comes to love relationships.

HOW SMART LOVE WORKS

Most people put more time and energy into planning a dinner party or shopping for a car than they do seeking a mate who is right for them. Unfortunately, there are serious consequences when romance is left entirely to chance. Oh, we know, it sounds so businesslike to talk "strategy" when it comes to dating. "You should just let it happen," we often hear. But that's a cop-out. If you're going to date smart you have to think smart.

Have you considered the kinds of things you want in a dating relationship? What qualities are you looking for in another person? What traits, skills, abilities would fit the bill for you? Whether you've made your "shopping list" or not, we've got to tell you that it may be deceiving. Unless you are practicing smart love, what you think you're looking for may be off the mark.

Thirty years ago when college students were asked to rank the attributes that are important to them in a potential date, they almost never put looks at the top of the list. But what they said was not always consistent with what they did. In a classic study where more than seven hundred college students were matched at a "computer dance," the researchers assessed each student's intelligence, aptitude, social skills, personality traits, and physical attractiveness. During an intermission at the dance, and again a few months later, the students were asked in private how much they liked their dates. The only variable that predicted their answers was attractiveness.[4]

Today's students are a little more honest, if not superficial. When asked to indicate the most important quality in a dating partner, they don't hesitate. "Looks" is the first word they utter.[5] So let's all be honest, the secret's out: whether we admit it or not, physical attractiveness tops the list of desirable dating qualities. Is this wrong? Absolutely not. Sex appeal is part of God's design. But here's the clincher: there's far more to a dating relationship than looks. The truth is physical attractiveness is a good spring, but a poor regulator. It gets love going but it doesn't *keep* love going.

> Love built on beauty, soon as beauty, dies.
>
> —∱ John Donne

Smart love understands this and looks beneath the surface. Smart love looks beyond beauty to find sustaining principles for lasting love, a love that may uphold lifelong marriage. After all, the divorce rate is so high, according to Yale researcher Robert Sternberg, not because people make foolish choices, but because they are drawn together for reasons that matter less as time goes on.[6] In other words, the force that brings a couple together—physical attractiveness—has little to do with what keeps them together. For too long, couples have based the start of their relationship on superficialities and then hoped for the best. But there's a better way. You no longer need to leave the future of your relationship to chance.

So stop torturing daisies—there's a whole new way to rate your love life. It has to do with playing it smart; it has to do with raising your love I.Q. Here's how it works.

Smart Love Seeks a Good Match

We've all heard it: Opposites attract. But is it true? Hardly. In reality, opposites seldom attract, and if they do they often don't stay attracted. The old "birds of a feather" thing may sound trite, but it's the truth. Close relationships are more likely to form and endure with someone who shares your ideas, values, and desires, a person who likes the same music, the same activities, even the same foods. For good reason the prophet Amos wondered, "Can two walk together, except they be agreed?"[7]

How do you know if you have a lot in common? It takes time. And it doesn't hurt to withhold premature judgments. We have a friend who says she dates "like Margaret Mead." On a promising date she brings along her anthropological, oh-isn't-that-interesting self, observing and recording differences "as if the guy were an alien species." By considering the first few dates as an expedition, she's learned to listen more and react less. And it pays off. She doesn't jump to critical conclusions because he isn't willing to try Thai food or has a different political view from hers. Over time, she patiently sifts through the dating data to discover whether she and her date are a good match on the things that matter most.

Differences emerge in any close relationship, of course. But smart love knows that for a fighting chance the relation-

> A man falls in love through his eyes, a woman through her ears.
>
> —⚡ Woodrow Wyatt

ship must be built on common ground. In one famous study of more than three hundred dating couples in Boston, those who eventually broke up were less well-matched in age, educational ambitions, intelligence, and physical attractiveness than those who stayed together.[8] Study after study has found little support for the "opposites attract" idea. Instead, the happiest couples are those with lots of similarities.[9] To paraphrase Henry Ward Beecher, "A well-matched couple is winged, an ill-matched couple is shackled."

●◇ Exercise 22: Are You a Good Match?

How can you tell if you are well-matched with the person you are dating? It may not be as difficult as you would guess. This exercise in the *Relationships Workbook* will help you assess whether or not you are in sync with a particular date.

Smart Love Pays Attention to Values

Five dates into her "last worst relationship," Cameron overheard Jess on the telephone, screaming at his mother. "I said to myself, he'd never talk to *me* that way." One year later, says Cameron, that was about the only way he *did* talk to her. No big surprise to learn the relation-ship self-destructed.

The person you date is constantly giving out clues about his or her values. And if you're smart, you'll pay attention. Why? Because what a person values reveals the course of your relationship and how you will be treated. If your date respects his younger sister, chances are he'll respect you too—it's part of his value system. How a person treats fam-ily and friends, however, is just one area where values are revealed.

You'll also want to pay attention to how that person treats him or herself. Does she see herself as the victim? Is he always blaming oth-ers? Money is another realm of revelation when it comes to values. Is this person wise with financial decisions? Generous? How about this per-son's commitments? Does he keep his promises? Is she reliable? What about this person's spiritual values? Does he talk about spiritual issues? Is she on a spiritual quest?

You discover what people value by paying attention to what makes them laugh, what they fear, what they desire, and how they spend their time. And the more you know about their values, the smarter you become about the future of your relationship.

Smart Love Doesn't Try to Change Others

Alfred Hitchcock's 1956 movie *Vertigo* startles the audience with several scary scenes, but none is as terrifying as when Kim Novak pre-sents her remade self to Jimmy Stewart. She is dressed in a gray suit and a white blouse, and her hair is done up in a seascape of blond waves. What's so frightening? Stewart has wholly recreated her in the image of a dead woman he had loved. By making her over he thinks that he has bought a second chance at happiness, but as the plot twists, we realize he has doomed them both.

Doom awaits any rela-tionship where one person is trying to change the other into something or someone they

> We have been seamed, not grafted.
> Though our steps interlock, each dances
> his own dance.
>
> —Lucy Shaw

aren't. And yet that is exactly what dumb love does. We can't tell you
how many people we've counseled who believe they can "fix" their date.
They are so desperate to be in a relationship they delude themselves
into believing a lie—that the flaws they now see in this person will
somehow evaporate under the influence of their love. But the flaws
remain. Here's the truth smart lovers know: What you see is what you
get, and your chances of changing it are very slim.

When talking with someone who believes they can change
another person we sometimes ask them to think how difficult it is to
lose three pounds to slightly improve their appearance. They generally concede the struggle. We then ask, "Now, what's the likelihood
of changing an entire personality?"

Let's make this perfectly clear: A person who recognizes flaws in
his or her mate during courtship and vows to do a remake after marriage
is simply looking for trouble. Smart love knows better.

Smart Love Doesn't Try to Change Oneself

Not only does smart love not attempt to change another person,
it knows better than to try and change oneself for another person.
Twenty-three-year old Judy, unfortunately, hadn't learned this lesson.
When she met Don she couldn't believe her eyes. "He was gorgeous,"
she told us. "He had everything—good looks, self-confidence, a good
job, a sense of humor—and I couldn't believe he was asking me out
on a date." She went on to tell us how her girlfriend's mother worked
in the same office building with Don and could supply "the inside
scoop" on him.

Judy learned that Don loved sailing and played saxophone in a jazz
band. She learned he had traveled extensively in India. With this and
other advanced knowledge of Don, Judy confessed to "brushing up" on
her knowledge of sailing, jazz, India, and all things Don. So what's the
problem with doing a little research? Nothing, really. The problem
emerged when on their first date Judy found herself not only being
knowledgeable about their "common" interests, but making up little

> If love ... means that one person absorbs the other, then no real relationship exists any more. Love evaporates; there is nothing left to love. The integrity of self is gone.
>
> —⚡ Annie Oakley

white lies to woo him. "I love Dizzy Gillespie," she enthusiastically told Don—a day earlier she hadn't even known who he was. Judy, knowing next to nothing about Indian food, told Don it was her favorite. You can probably guess what happened next. Don thought he had found his soul mate—"It's almost spooky how much we have in common," he told her.

Spooky, indeed. A few dates later, the whole relationship fell apart. That's when Judy walked into our office and confessed a string of similar failed relationships with great potential partners where she became whoever she thought her date wanted her to be. Like a chameleon changing colors to blend in, Judy would contort her likes and dislikes, her whole personality, if she thought it would make her more alluring. It's no wonder Judy couldn't maintain an ongoing dating relationship. No one can if they are not true to themselves.

Judy's pressure to change herself came from within, but we have met plenty of people who felt the same pressure to change from the person they are dating. In either case, being true to yourself is still paramount. If you find you have to alter yourself considerably to fit in with his or her friends, for example, you've discovered a danger sign, and it reads, "This isn't going to work." Be courageous and move on. "It is better to be hated for what you are," said André Gide, "than loved for what you are not."

●◆ Exercise 23: The True You Self-Test

One of the healthiest things you can do for your dating relationships is to be who you really are. This exercise in the *Relationships Workbook* will help you determine whether you are easily influenced by external pressures or whether you are more likely to stand firm in your own convictions of the kind of person you are and want to be.

Smart Love Doesn't Play Games

Let the male take the lead and carry the conversation. Be honest but mysterious—men like a challenge. Don't return all his calls, and never stay on the phone with him longer than ten minutes. Always be the one who ends a date or a phone call. Never accept a Saturday date if he asks later than Wednesday. Break off the relationship immediately if no gift arrives on your birthday or Valentine's Day. Rarely say thank you for presents.

> Whenever I want a really nice meal, I start dating again.
>
> —Susan Healy

There are thirty-five of these sorts of rules in all, according to the Cosmopolitan-style magazine article gussied up as a book that has achieved bestsellerdom. *The Rules,* by Ellen Fein and Sherrie Schneider, has also achieved cult status, spawning seminars and support groups around the country. For $250 an hour, fans can get direct phone advice from the authors. The point of the whole thing? Play by the rules and you win Mr. Right. Perhaps. The question we ask is for how long? How long are you willing to play the game? Carry out the charade? Sooner or later the real you will emerge, and then what?

Rules are for games, not relationships. And smart love knows the difference. Games are meant to lure, even manipulate another person into seeing you as someone you're not. We're not picking on this little book of codified dating advice. The games people play in dating relationships are nothing new. They're as old as time. As is the damage they cause. Anytime you project an image that is not real, you are hiding your true self and playing a game you'll eventually lose. You may win attention, sympathy, or admiration for the moment, but it won't last— it's only a game.

So if you're looking for love that goes the distance, you've got to avoid game playing as much as possible and be real. Consider the childhood game of hide and seek. "Oh, the delicious thrill of hiding while the others come looking for you," writes French author Jean Baudrillard, "the delicious terror of being discovered, but what panic when, after a long search, the others abandon you!"[10] Dating games, played too much and too long, result in the same aloneness. So play a few games if you must, but don't hide too well. Our advice? We'll say it again, be who you are and the dates will follow.

Smart Love Doesn't Run from Conflict

He didn't follow through on his promise to pick you up at an agreed upon time. She said something embarrassing in front of your friends and you lost it. Whatever the issue, wherever the place, your first fight is inevitable. And you feel devastated. Scared. Disillusioned. Worried that you've ruined everything. Well, rest assured, you haven't. Only dumb love runs from the slightest conflict. Smart love uses the harsh words and hurt feelings to better understand each other and the relationship.

> Love is an act of endless forgiveness, a tender look which becomes a habit.
> —√ Peter Ustinov

Four weeks into their romance, Todd failed to invite Patricia to a fancy dinner sponsored by his company. Patricia felt hurt but kept it to herself. After all, their relationship was still brand-new. At seven weeks Todd went solo to his high school reunion. Patricia felt annoyed. They'd been dating steadily. Were they not a couple? At three months, Todd told Patricia that he was spending Thanksgiving in California with his former college roommate, not in Seattle with his family and her. "That was when I went ballistic," says Patricia. This fledgling couple had their first real fight, complete with yelling and crying.

Afterward, they each went home and replayed the fight a thousand times in their heads—until Patricia called Todd. The rest of the night and into the next day, the two of them had their first real conversation about their relationship, about where they each hoped and feared it might go. Todd admitted some resistance to being definitively "coupled" but stressed that the relationship was meaningful to him and he wanted to move it forward.

At the end of their talk, Todd and Patricia felt exhausted and a little fragile. But they also felt closer. "I learned more about who Todd was in this one fight than I had in months of dating." Patricia knows they'll eventually argue again, but she also understands that they can use conflict to their advantage. Patricia's no dummy.

Smart Love Knows the Bottom Line

When Gary and Brenda first met, their dates mostly happened like this: If Gary wanted to see Brenda on the weekend, he called her sometime on Thursday to make plans for Saturday night; otherwise she didn't hear from him. After weeks of this, Brenda balked. "It felt too unbalanced. I had no control. If I wanted to see him, I had to wait, not make other plans." And so the Thursday eventually came when Brenda sweetly declared herself busy on Saturday. She turned down dates with Gary until eventually he got the message and changed his pattern.

It's a little thing, but it illustrates a big point: Smart love has standards of behavior in a relationship. Smart love has a bottom line that says, *This is what I can and cannot live with.* Whether it be about common courtesy, seeing other people, or having limits on sex, smart love preserves your dignity, integrity, and well-being.

Everyone's bottom line is different. We can't tell you where to draw the line on every issue. That's your decision. You call the shots about what you can and cannot live with. The point is to know what you want from a dating partner and where you are willing to bend—and where you are not.

Beware: If you are to hold to your bottom line, you must ultimately accept the possibility of being alone. You must be willing to walk if the relationship isn't allowing your best self to flourish. Here's the bottom line of smart love: A lousy relationship is never better than no relationship at all.

•❖ *Exercise 24: Determining Your Bottom Line*
Do you know exactly what you are willing to live with in a dating relationship? Have you determined what you absolutely will not put up with? This exercise in the *Relationships Workbook* will help you do just that. Take a moment to do this exercise, and you will better be able to rest in the security of knowing where you stand.

KEEPING THE LOVE OF YOUR LIFE

"All beginnings are lovely," a French proverb tells us. That's particularly true of a promising new dating relationship. But no matter how lovely, a beginning is only a beginning. Time will tell if a relationship is built to go the distance. And smart love, not leaving everything up to chance, can once again put the odds of survival in your favor. So we conclude this chapter with one more thought for anyone who has found true love and wants to keep it.

Here it is: love is not static. Love is not something you fall into and fall out of. Love is fluid. It rises and falls like the tide. "When you love someone," writes Anne Morrow Lindbergh in her little book *Gift from the Sea*, "you do not love them all the time, in exactly the same way, from moment to moment." It's impossible. Yet this is what dumb love demands. Smart love, on the other hand, has faith in the ebb and flow of love, knowing that it is fluid and free. Smart love works day to day at being in love. It doesn't sit back and get sucked under by the happily-ever-after myth. Smart love practices loving ways of being.

So if you are blessed with a healthy, budding love-relationship, don't set yourself up for disappointment by thinking your feelings of love are permanent. Don't leap at the flow of the tide, as Lindbergh says, and resist in terror its ebb. Be smart and know that love, no matter how lovely in the beginning, will change and change again.

FOR REFLECTION

- In specific terms, how would you describe the emotions surrounding infatuation and falling in love? Are they the same thing?

- Journalist Helen Rowland said, "Falling in love consists merely in uncorking the imagination and bottling the common sense." In what ways does falling in love impair our judgment and deplete our common sense?

- Do you agree that detecting your partner's values can be one of the smartest moves you make while dating? Why or why not? If you believe it is important, how do you go about discovering them?

- How have you tried to change another person to please you more? And how have you tried to change yourself to please another person? In both cases, what was the result?

- What "bottom lines" have you determined for yourself in dating other people? Do you need to communicate them to the person you are dating? If so, how do you do this?

chapter seven

Sex, Lies, and the Great Escape

Sex is no test of love, for it is precisely the very thing one wants to test that is destroyed by the testing.

—— Walter Trobisch

"Penis." "Vagina." "Penis." "Vagina." I (Les) couldn't believe these words were coming out of my mouth. One after the other, like an old-fashioned record stuck in one place. "Penis." "Vagina." I just kept saying them. Actually, I was being instructed to say them by a no-nonsense graduate professor while I was standing before a group of twenty Ph.D. students, all of them strangers. It was the first day of a course on human sexuality. With no introduction, the professor wrote her name on the board, turned to the class of psychologists-in-training, and said, "Sexuality makes most people uncomfortable, and you can't be a good psychologist if you get nervous talking about sex."

With those words, I could sense every student squirming uncomfortably, like sixth graders in a sex-education class. "Dr. Parrott, let's start with you," she said looking at her class roster. *Start with me and do what?* I wondered. *Anybody but me! Why start with me?* I wanted to run from the room or crawl under my chair at the very least. I wanted to escape. "Come to the front of the class," she said. My heart began to race, my face turned red, and beads of sweat instantly formed on my forehead.

> Sexuality throbs within us as movement toward relationship, intimacy, companionship.
>
> —⚡ Lewis Smedes

"How are you feeling?" the professor asked.

"Fine," I stuttered. "Just fine, thanks."

"Good," she said while looking at the other students. "That's very good. What I want you to do is maintain eye contact with Dr. Stewart over here and say the words *penis* and *vagina*."

There was nervous laughter and an air of disbelief throughout the classroom. Surely this was a joke. But it wasn't. One by one, the professor had every student stand before the group, make eye contact with each individual in the room while saying (apparently) her two favorite words. What a relief to be first and get it over with. After my turn, I went back to my seat, mopped the sweat from my brow, and tried to recuperate while every other student endured the same uncomfortable exercise.

The whole thing took more than thirty minutes. Looking back on it, however, the time was well spent. I mean, the professor was right: if you are going to be a good clinician, you've got to get over the normal anxiety we humans have of talking frankly about sex. The reason being is that sex is a part of who we are. And if that makes us nervous, we can't be whole. I learned a lot of things in that course, but the first day's lesson is one that will not soon leave me.

Well, you won't be forced to undergo any such exercise in this chapter. But if you stick with us through the next few pages, we aren't going to let you escape the sometimes uncomfortable issues and choices involving your own sexuality. We will tell you right up front that this chapter is dedicated to exposing two fundamental lies people want to believe in order to escape the truth about sex. The first lie is that we can't do anything to tame our animal instincts, and the second is that having sex will bolster our self-image by making us more desirable or more confident. Our goal is not to scare you into premarital chastity with horror stories of shame and disease. Neither is it to teach you how sperm meets egg and the importance of using condoms. No. This chapter takes an unconventional route.

We begin by showing how different we are from the birds and the bees—how we humans have an advantage over the animal kingdom when it comes to our sexual instincts. We then revisit our "compulsion for completion" in the sexual context by showing what lures both men and women toward the sex-too-soon syndrome. Much of the chapter is then given to helping you make wise choices about your sexuality so that you can enjoy it to the fullest. We'll be honest about why we think it's a good reason to "just say wait," and we'll give you some specific guidelines for recovering from sexual regret. We begin, however, with a popular refrain ... "birds do it, bees do it, even ordinary fleas do it."

BEYOND "DOING IT"

"Animal instinct." It's a phrase we often hear in the context of human sexuality. But the person who uses it must know very little about the bizarre and kinky habits of the natural world. Consider the evidence (adult discretion advised). You've probably heard that the female praying mantis will bite the head off the male while they are mating. But have you heard that the lower half of the male will continue to copulate even after its top half has been consumed? And what should we make of the barbaric female sea worm, who abruptly turns on an unsuspecting male and munches the tail right off in order to fertilize her eggs? One more cannibalistic creature, just to make the point. The name of the black widow spider suggests death, but who'd have thought that she'd cold-bloodedly devour up to twenty-five mates in one day?

Not all the animal kingdom is so unpleasant. Many male species will go to great lengths to impress the females. That includes the most romantic of rodents, the mole rat, who painstakingly constructs not only an elaborate subterranean house of halls, but also a special "wedding chamber" exclusively reserved for mating. Then there's the female red-eyed tree frog, who carries her mate around on her back, then lifts him over the threshold and sets him gently down to fertilize her eggs.

As far as cats go, they do their business in the night with so much scratching and screeching that it makes sex sound about as appealing as being locked in a room with a manicurist who files fingernails on a chalkboard. Dogs are a lot less discreet. They are likely to do the deed at any time of day to any kind of thing. Maybe that's what some people mean by the natural "animal instinct" in humans. They mean it's just involuntary, reflexive. So they "do it."

The truth is that human sexuality is worlds apart from the birds and bees. The difference? It's found in the most important sexual organ we humans have: our brains. The human sexual drive operates out of the "cortex," that thin outer layer of the brain where all learning takes place. Humans use their highly developed brains to learn how, when, where, and whether they will give expression to their sexual urges—it's what separates us from the animals. In other words, because we are human we are responsible for our sexuality. We have the power—even when our biochemistry battles our brain—to make choices. We are more than our hormones. Unlike an animal's brain, our cortex allows us to control our urges.

> Not to have control over the senses is like sailing in a rudderless ship, bound to break to pieces on coming in contact with the very first rock.
>
> —Mahatma Gandhi

Still not convinced of our power to control sexual urges? Consider a male gynecologist who can clinically examine female sexual organs all day long without any sexual reaction and yet get aroused when he goes home and sees his wife in her nightgown. The reason: brainpower.

All this is not to diminish the human sex drive. It is admittedly powerful—right from the beginning. A little boy has his first erection within minutes after birth, and a little girl has her first vaginal lubrication within hours after birth. We are sexual beings. There's no denying it. Sexuality is an integral part of who we are. It's how God made us. Even as a single person, there is no way you cannot be sexual. But we'll say it again: Just because you are sexual does not mean you are doomed to be the victim of your raging hormones. Just because you are sexual doesn't mean you have to fall prey to the animal instinct of "doing it."

●◆ Exercise 25: Your Most Important Sex Organ

What do you really believe about your ability to control yourself in those seemingly uncontrollable situations? Do you have what it takes? This exercise in the *Relationships Workbook* will help you think through your capacity to use your most important sex organ when you need it the most.

THE JOY OF WHAT?

If we humans have the cognitive capacity, the cerebral equipment, to control our sexual impulses, why is our sexuality so often the source of our problems? Why are we not more intentional and deliberate about our sexual urges? Why are there so many affairs, venereal diseases, unwanted pregnancies, and abortions? Why so many broken hearts and sexual shipwrecks?

The fantasy factory of Hollywood can't be ignored in trying to answer these questions. Consider some of the most highly ranked shows in recent years. On *Friends*, Phoebe has a problem: her boyfriend won't sleep with her. "The guy still won't put out, huh?" a pal commiserates. The gang speculates he must be gay. Later, she can barely contain her glee: she finally "made it" with her boyfriend. The trick, she explains, was to make clear to him that she wasn't expecting a commitment just because they'd had sex. On *Melrose Place*, an inebriated Jake takes a stranger to his hotel room. "No strings attached, right?" he asks her. "None but these," she says, dropping the spaghetti straps of her slip from her shoulders by way of an answer. And on *Seinfeld*, a minicrisis erupts because of a shortage of contraceptive sponges. With supplies limited, Elaine interviews her date to decide if he is "spongeworthy."

> Sex has become one of the most discussed subjects of modern times. The Victorians pretended it did not exist; the moderns pretend that nothing else exists.
>
> —Fulton J. Sheen

Examples of cavalier sexual acts on sitcoms and hour-long dramas (to say nothing of radio, movies, and music videos) are endless. Recent studies reveal that only one in eighty-five sexual references on TV concerned birth control, abortion, or sexually transmitted diseases.[1] Need we say more? It should be plain: When night after night in our own homes sexuality is portrayed without any serious consequences, there are going to be real-life casualties. Ironically, Bart Simpson, the cartoon character, summed it up nicely. "It's just hard not listening to TV," he told his father. "It's spent more time raising us than you have."

Okay. So it's well known that the media is in the business of manufacturing myths about our sex lives. But can we place all the blame on Tinsel Town? Not if we're honest. The real reason for having sex-too-soon is found within each individual and it stems from what we call the compulsion for completion (see chapter 1). If we are in a romantic relationship without the foundation of a solid sense of self-worth—without knowing who we are and what we want—we are playing with fire.

The danger is almost predicated by your gender. If you're an insecure woman, for example, the primary question you're probably asking is "Am I desirable?" You see sex as a barometer of your worthiness and as a means to relational connectedness.

We have a friend in Virginia who is the director of a home for unwed mothers. One day as Julie was giving us a tour of her gleaming facilities, she pointed out that the adolescent women who were there had by and large turned to sexual experimentation out of a frantic longing to be wanted—to be desirable. Sex became their way of getting the cuddling and acceptance that was missing in their family.

"Having sex to me," a twenty-something college student recently confessed in our office, "was a sign that I was wanted by someone else." She described intercourse with her boyfriend as "proof" that she was attractive and desirable. It helped her shake off a haunting sense of personal inadequacy and low self-esteem. Wanting to be desirable, of course, is not a bad thing. It's only a problem when it's motivated out of inadequacy and it becomes a thirst you're willing to satisfy at any cost—including being used in exchange for sweet talk and a fleeting feeling of passionate love.

For men the primary sexual question is often "Am I capable?" The insecure male tends to see sex in terms of power and performance, competition and achievement. For him, it can even become a numbers game. Remember the Spur Posse from a middle-class suburb in Los Angeles? There's hardly a more dramatic example. It hit the headlines when deputies arrested eight members of a high school boys' clique made up of athletes whose main activity was "hooking up," or having sex, with as many girls as possible. The athletes kept scorecards and gleefully compared and boasted about their scores. The town of Lakewood, California has been divided against itself ever since. While most citizens have been appalled by the sexual activities of the group, a few fathers have actually defended the boys. "It's a rite of passage, a part of growing up and becoming a man," one father said. At the Belman home, where son Kristopher, eighteen, had returned after being released from custody, his father said, "Nothing my boy did was anything any red-blooded American boy wouldn't do at his age." No wonder the boys saw no cause for remorse. "My dad used to brag to his friends," one of them said. "All the dads did. . . . It's the moms that are freaking out about this stuff. But that's probably that Freudian thing. You know, penis envy."[2]

Sound unusual? It's not. Insecure men have long looked to their sexual prowess as a means to becoming more "manly." Some men don't look to the number of women as much as their age. And we're not only talking about Joey Buttafuocco and Amy Fisher, Woody Allen and

> Our passions are like convulsion fits, which, though they make us stronger for the time, leave us the weaker ever after.
>
> —Jonathan Swift

Soon-Yi Previn or the fact that O. J. Simpson was thirty when he began dating an eighteen-year-old waitress named Nicole Brown. Federal and state surveys suggest that adult males are the fathers of some two-thirds of the babies born to teenage girls.

Before we move on, we want to make this point perfectly clear: Sex-too-soon will never validate you or your relationship. If you're a woman, it won't make you feel more desirable. If you're a man, it won't dismantle your insecurity. Sex-too-soon will actually do the opposite. It will end up making you feel more self-denigrated, desperate, alone, and insecure. So what's a sexual being to do? We're glad you asked.

WHAT ARE YOUR CHOICES?

We recently spent an entire day, breakfast through dinner, with sex therapists Clifford and Joyce Penner from Pasadena, California. You may know them from their best-selling book, *The Gift of Sex* or *Getting Your Sex Life Off to a Great Start*. The Penners have been counseling people on sexual struggles for more than two decades and have heard every conceivable story you can imagine on the topic. They have devoted their professional lives to helping people enjoy sexuality to the fullest. They understand the mechanics of what makes sex good and why it sometimes goes painfully wrong. But they also know that good sex involves far more than biology. The Penners underscore the emotional and spiritual aspects of a vital sexual relationship, not just in the heat of the moment but long after the fire has died down. And when we asked the Penners why so many of the young adults we see are suffering from the sex-too-soon syndrome, they almost answered in unison: "It comes down to choices." They told us that the number-one reason people end up in their office for counseling is to repair the emotional and spiritual damage of their choices—the ones they made or didn't make.

In the heat of passion, people aren't thinking about the long-term consequences of their choices. "By that time," says Joyce Penner, "the blood has already rushed from their head." The time to make informed choices about your sexuality is now, and we want to help you make the choice that best fits your values. We want to show you how different choices impact not only your present relationships, but how they will affect you and your partner down the road. So here are the five most common choices people make about having sex. Think about them. Then make up your own mind.

The "It-Just-Happened" Choice

Lauren and her boyfriend walked to his apartment after a few hours of studying in the college library. Before Mike opened the door, he grinned teasingly and said, "My roommate's gone for the night." Lauren tensed as he nudged her into his living room. Before she'd even taken off her jacket, Mike was kissing her. "You are so gorgeous tonight," he whispered. "I care about you so much, and I want you to know it." Lauren's mind was whirling. She searched his eyes and nodded without thinking as he led her to his bedroom.

"Mike believed in me when no one else would," she later told us. "I wasn't planning to have sex with him that night, but I knew the future of our relationship would probably be over if we weren't intimate soon." During the next few months Lauren became consumed with Mike. "He was all that mattered," as she put it. Sex soon became part of all their dates. But when Lauren began talking about changing her summer plans to be with Mike, his passion quickly cooled. "I'd changed the course of my whole life by saying yes to his sexual advances, and now he was retreating because I was changing my summer plans." It was no real surprise that Lauren and Mike broke up before the end of spring semester.

Unplanned sex may feel right at the time, but it almost always ushers in the end of the relationship. Why? Because when you do not consciously make a decision about something as important as sex, you surrender your being to winds of chance. And no relationship can survive on that.

National studies show that only seventeen percent of young women say they planned their first sexual intercourse—meaning most apparently have sex because it "just happens" in the heat of passion.[3] The lesson to be learned from this "choice" is that if you don't actively make a choice that *is* your choice, your chances of having sex-too-soon skyrocket.

The "If-We're-in-Love-It-Can't-Be-Wrong" Choice

Let's consider Lauren's story from Mike's perspective. He sees what happened that night in his apartment quite differently. After dating for more than four months, he and Lauren had grown very close and talked openly about many intimate issues. Mike, for example, knew about Lauren's turbulent and sometimes borderline-abusive relationship with her father. And Lauren knew the details of Mike's last disastrous breakup with his ex-girlfriend. As Mike put it, Lauren and he knew each other's hearts. They cared deeply for each other. They had also enjoyed what Mike referred to as "the world's greatest marathon make-out sessions." He told us they could lose all track of time in their "sessions," but they never came close to having intercourse. He admitted he'd thought about it many times, but neither of them spoke about going all the way. "We never talked about limits or anything," he said. "I just figured that the more we came to love each other, the more intimate we would be." He also told us that on one occasion he brought up the idea of taking a bath with Lauren and she "just giggled."

All this nebulous and flirtatious talk and behavior gave Mike the idea that as they were falling in love, sex would be a natural expression of their love. "In my line of thinking," Mike said, "sex is a way of expressing feelings you can't express with words. Believe me, I'm not the kind of guy who is looking for a one-night stand; I'm not going to jump in the sack with just anybody." He told us how "honoring" women

was important to him and that
he would never "use" a woman
to get sex.

> Passion, though a bad regulator, is a powerful spring.
> —⟶ Ralph Waldo Emerson

It's tempting to believe
that love sanctifies sex. But
that's a fallacy. Sex, even in the context of a caring and loving relationship, will forever change the dynamics of that relationship. Sexual
intercourse draws us into the profound mystery of a "one-flesh" reality. It is meant to unite and bond in a deep and wonderful way. But
there's a hitch. Sex outside the lifelong covenant of permanence and
fidelity sets up expectations and creates needs that almost always dismantle the relationship.

"It's weird," Mike told us. "Once Lauren wanted to change her
summer plans just to be with me I began to feel smothered. She was
making this big commitment, and I wasn't ready for that." No matter
how loving he believed himself to be, the truth is—Mike wasn't ready
for sex either.

The "Sex-Brings-Us-Closer-Together" Choice

At the end of the exhilarating, action-packed movie *Speed*, Keanu
Reeves says to Sandra Bullock, "I've heard that relationships based on
intense experiences never work." Bullock replies, "Okay, we'll have to
base it on sex." When we asked a group of college students in Kentucky recently what they thought of Bullock's statement, most agreed
it was ridiculous. "If your relationship is based on sex," one of them said,
"you don't *have* a relationship." We couldn't agree more. But we've also
met plenty of single people who choose sex because they are in love and
having sex brings them closer together. They behave as if they are married, preparing for regular sexual encounters together on their dates.

A sincere churchgoing couple in their mid-twenties told us that,
as Christians, they both felt they shouldn't have sex before marriage.
But in the heat of passion, just two months into their relationship, they
had intercourse and have never regretted it. "Well, we felt guilty at

first," one of them confided, "but we realized over the last three months that we were now more in love with each other than ever." They told us how having guilt-free sex helped them love each other all the more.

Sex *can* bring two people closer together—for a time. The problem with using sex as a means to more intimacy is that it soon becomes a substitute for emotional intimacy itself. Couples who put their sexuality on fast forward short-circuit the normal progression of linking their hearts and souls. Research shows that the emotional bonding required for lasting love is most likely to move systematically and slowly through specific stages (see Exercise 26). Using sex to speed up that process doesn't work; not for the long haul.[4] A relationship that is to achieve its full potential requires emotional vulnerability and countless private memories unknown to the rest of the world. Sex-too-soon keeps that from happening. It creates an illusion of intimacy that fades with the fires of passion. "There is so much use of the body as a substitute for psychological intimacy," says psychologist Rollo May. "It's much easier to jump in bed with someone than it is to share your fears and anxieties." So don't delude yourself into thinking that sex brings you closer together in any lasting or meaningful way. It doesn't.

•❖ Exercise 26: The Bonds That Bind

Have you explored your own thinking on how to establish long-lasting physical bonds in a relationship? Do you know what happens when specific and predictable stages are short-circuited? This exercise in the *Relationships Workbook* will help you clarify your thinking on the bonds that bind and sometimes backfire.

The "I'm-Not-Sexual-Until-I'm-Married" Choice

The automatic choice for some sincere single people is to shut down—completely—all of their sexual feelings to avoid even the slightest temptation of sex before marriage. They don't hug, they don't kiss, they may not even hold hands except in public. We know a recently married couple who made this choice together. When they proclaimed their purity at the ceremony, I whispered to Leslie, "I hope their bodies haven't forgotten what to do on the honeymoon." I wasn't saying this to be flippant. I was being serious. When a person completely buries their sexuality, when they block all sensuousness from their relationship, they run the risk of making sex something out of control or even dirty. They say to themselves that good people don't enjoy sex, and as a result they feel cheap and sinful when they do have sex, even if it's married sex.

Anyone who seeks to destroy the passions instead of controlling them is trying to play the angel.

—⚡ Voltaire

Someone once remarked that many of us were taught: "Sex is dirty. Save it for the person you marry." When it's put that way, it's easy to see the absurdity and contradiction in such teachings. Yet many swallow such admonitions without allowing themselves to think about their full and lasting impact. Years into marriage, these couples are often not permitting themselves to accept their sexuality. They feel restrained or even guilty over having sex with their husband or wife.

Cliff and Joyce Penner have told us that in their work as sex therapists they have seen countless couples who had chosen to be asexual only to discover as they moved into marriage that they had no desire for one another. "Sexuality does not work this way," according to the Penners. "It is an innate appetite, just like hunger. People can control how much they eat, just as they can control their sexual behavior. But when they shut down their appetites for food they become anorexic; likewise, if they turn off their sexual feelings they become sexually apathetic."

You can control your passion without denying your sexuality. Kissing, hugging, and hand holding are ways of showing mutual endearment and tender caring. They can be part of a wholesome dating relationship. And they can be enjoyed for their own sake without leading to sexual intercourse. Sex is not a wild bronco you can't control and it's not dirty—it's not even a four-letter word.

The "Let's-Set-Boundaries" Choice

Whenever someone asks us if we believe in premarital sex we respond by saying "yes and no." It's a confusing answer at first, but it gives us an opportunity to make an important point. God affirms our sexuality as human beings and we can't suddenly become asexual; we can't deny or ignore completely the sexual part of ourselves before we are married without suffering severe consequences. For this reason, we believe in premarital sexuality. We are quick to follow up, however, by saying that having genital sex before marriage is clearly not in line with God's principles. Sexual intercourse is a "life-uniting act," as our friend Lewis Smedes calls it. That's why sex outside of marriage is "sex-to-soon." It violates the intended purpose of sex. "It is wrong," according to Smedes, "because unmarried people thereby engage in a life-uniting act without a life-uniting intent. . . . Intercourse signs and seals— and maybe even delivers—a life-union; and life union means marriage."[5]

So if you want to reserve sexual intercourse for marriage, the $100 question is *how*? How do you abstain from sex without shutting off your sexuality? Granted, it's not easy, it can be down right excruciating— but it's possible. We know plenty of happy couples who have saved sex for marriage. In case you are wondering, we abstained from premarital sex ourselves. In seven years of dating we had our share of passionate moments and plenty of tempting situations, but we stayed true to our decision to wait. Looking back over our entire relationship, it remains as one of the best decisions we ever made. We had plenty of time to evolve through the natural stages of physical intimacy as our permanent commitment to each other progressed.

The secret to saving sex for marriage is found in a single word: boundaries. Couples who abstain from sex without shutting off their sexuality have learned to set specific boundaries and stick to them. They have made intentional, deliberate, and conscious choices about how far they will go. They have considered the following scale of physical contact and drawn a line:

THE PHYSICAL INTIMACY SCALE

1. Embracing and hand holding
2. Cuddling and gentle caressing
3. Polite kissing on the lips
4. Passionate total mouth kissing
5. Intense and prolonged total mouth kissing
6. Fondling breasts and genitals outside the clothes
7. Fondling breasts and genitals under the clothes
8. Oral or genital stimulation to orgasm outside the clothes
9. Oral or genital stimulation to orgasm under the clothes
10. Genital intercourse

We could tell you in specific terms where we think you should set your boundaries. We could point out that anytime you move past stage five it becomes exponentially more difficult to maintain control. But telling you what to do makes little difference unless you hold the belief with conviction. We can't be your conscience. This is a decision that requires serious thinking, clear understanding of where your values are based, and quite a bit of soul-searching on your part. You need to carefully consider what you and the person you are dating mutually agree is acceptable, given your values and goals. You need to decide exactly what is off-limits when it comes to physical touch, and you need to decide what settings (being alone in an apartment together, for example) are off-limits when it comes to making out. You also need to consider the kinds of clothes you wear on a date and whether they might make sticking to your decision more difficult.

Setting boundaries is a decision you need to make on your own and eventually talk over with your partner. You both need to know what the boundaries are. Exercise 27 will help you along the way. One more thing about setting boundaries. Once you set them, don't accelerate them for several months. And if, over time, you feel you must draw a more liberal line, never do it in the dark. Always set your boundaries in daylight with a cool head and a clear mind.

•• Exercise 27: Drawing the Line
   If you are smart, you will give careful consideration to
exactly how far you will go when it comes to physical intimacy, and you will take the necessary precautions to stick to
your decision. This exercise in the *Relationships Workbook* will
help you draw your line and not cross over it.

A FEW GOOD REASONS TO JUST SAY "WAIT"

If you are doubting the benefits of saving sex for marriage, allow us
to briefly summarize a few findings. Did you know a recent survey found
that the highest levels of sexual satisfaction are linked to marriage and
traditional sexual ethics?[6] That is, the people most apt to report that
they are very satisfied with their current sex life are not singles who
freely flit from one sexual encounter to another, but married couples
who "strongly" believe sex outside of marriage is wrong. In fact, "tra-
ditionalists" rank an astounding thirty-one percentage points higher
in their level of sexual satisfaction than singles who have no objection
to sex outside of marriage. The findings contribute to a growing body of
research linking sexual satisfaction to marital harmony, fidelity, and
permanence.[7]

These researchers found not only that sex is better in marriage,
but it is best if you have had only one sexual partner in a lifetime.
"Physical and emotional satisfaction started to decline when people
had more than one sexual partner," the researchers stated.[8] A study
at the University of South Carolina revealed that people who engaged
in premarital sex were more likely to be involved in extramarital affairs
once they were married.[9] David Larson, a senior researcher with the
National Institute of Health, in a review of existing research summed
it up this way: "Couples not involved before marriage and faithful during marriage are more satisfied with their current sex life and also with
their marriages compared to those who were involved sexually before
marriage."[10]

And did you know that research from Washington State University revealed, "Cohabiting couples compared to married couples have less healthy relationships"?[11] Researchers at UCLA explained that "cohabitors experienced significantly more difficulty in [subsequent] marriages with adultery . . . than couples who had not cohabited."[12] In fact, marriages preceded by living together are fifty percent more likely to break up than those marriages where couples did not.[13]

> *Hell is the only place outside heaven where we can be safe from the dangers of love.*
>
> —C. S. Lewis

Abstinence, research has clearly shown, makes the heart grow fonder.[14] But long before studies and statistics pointed to the practical reasons for saving sex for marriage, biblical wisdom[15] tried to steer us clear of the emotional aftermath of having sex-too-soon. The Bible doesn't say premarital sex is wrong just to test our self-discipline. We too often view God's principles as a list of rules set up to test our determination. The Bible says premarital intercourse is wrong for our own protection, because sex-too-soon is certain to hurt us. Ask anyone who's broken up with someone they slept with.

"The thing that really bugs me is that I gave him a part of me and now it's gone," a lovely college senior told me (Leslie) recently. "We weren't doing it every day, like some of my friends," she continued while struggling with tears. "I just wish I'd waited. I want something permanent before having sex again, some true love and a life commitment." It was a tender and lurching confession, full of pathos and pain. Like many young people we have talked to, she was retreating from sex not simply out of a fear of AIDS or a fear of God, but out of regret, self-blame, and most of all pain. Research, God's loving mandates, and the potential for personal pain should be reasons enough to just say wait.

LIKE A VIRGIN, AGAIN

Wilt Chamberlain, the former pro basketball star, bragged in his biography about sleeping with more than twenty thousand women.

Whether or not he's exaggerating doesn't really matter. His point is that sex is readily available, round the clock, for professional athletes. They call these women "groupies," and they hang out for a quick thrill wherever these teams travel. More impressive than Chamberlain's boastings about these women, however, is the decision A. C. Green made when he entered the NBA: to be a virgin until he married. Why? "Because," says A. C., "one, it's what God wants me to do. Two, it's what I want to do. And three, because I'm going to save my body for the person who really counts."[16]

Good for him, you may be thinking. *But I've already blown it.* Well, you're not alone.[17] If you've already given away your virginity, however, it's not too late to reclaim it.

Sometime ago, I (Les) was invited to sit in on a private discussion with a small group of men in a college residence hall. All of them were seniors about to graduate, and a couple were engaged to be married that summer. "One of the reasons we formed this group," a young man explained, "is that each of us wants to be able to look our wife in the face on our wedding night and say, 'I saved myself for you.'" Another spoke up and said the group gives them a sense of accountability to keep their commitment to abstinence. But then one of the group members revealed something I wasn't expecting: "All of us have had sex before, either in high school or in college, so we are kinda like neo-virgins." Neo-virgins! I'd never heard that term before, but I liked it immediately and I understood what he meant.

● Exercise 28: Healing the Hurt of Sexual Regret

Are you wondering how you can be set free from your mistakes and experience healthy loving relationships? Are you wondering if you can ever be forgiven and get rid of feelings of guilt and regret? This exercise in the *Relationships Workbook* will help you do just that by showing you a seven-step plan.

If you have sexual regrets and want to start with a clean slate, we are confident that you can walk beyond those regrets toward healthy relationships and guard yourself from having sex-too-soon again. "'Come now, let us reason together,' says the Lord. 'Though your sins are like scarlet, they shall be as white as snow.'"[18] Maybe you feel trapped by guilt, shame, frustration, loss of respect, and distrust. You can move beyond that. Maybe you have experienced a devastating breakup, venereal disease, an unwanted pregnancy, or an abortion. You can move beyond that too. In the midst of all the negative consequences and feelings from your sex-too-soon experience, there is hope. The bonded reality of intercourse is not utterly irreversible. But it does demand healing. To engage in a life-uniting act without a life-uniting intent wounds the inner spirit. Exercise 28 will help you get started on the healing journey and help you set a new course for saving sex for marriage. If you want to restore purity to your love life, it's possible.

FOR REFLECTION

- On a one-to-ten scale, with one being "none" and ten being "a lot," how much control do you think we have over our sexual impulses and why?
- Think back to the "compulsion for completion" concept discussed in chapter 1. How do you see this play out when it comes to our sexuality? How does our desire to be whole affect our sex lives? Does it differ for men and women, and if so how?
- Considering the five fundamental choices we have when it comes to having sex, which one makes the most sense to you and why? Have you, or do you know others who have fallen for unhealthy choices (e.g., "if we're in love it can't be wrong")? Why are these choices so seductive?
- What do you think about the whole idea of drawing a line when it comes to sexual behavior on a date? Is it reasonable to think that a couple can make a decision about how far they will go and then stick to it when the heat is on? Why or why not?

- If you were explaining to another person a few good reasons to save sex for marriage, what would you say? What would you say to the person who was no longer a virgin and was wondering whether they could reclaim their sexual purity?

chapter eight

Breaking Up Without Falling Apart

*There is hardly an activity, any enterprise, which is started
with such tremendous hopes and expectations
and yet which fails so regularly as love.*

—Erich Fromm

"We need to talk"—four of the most intimidating little words in a couple's vocabulary. And as soon as I heard Leslie utter them, I knew something big was brewing. We were three months into our engagement and six months away from our wedding. Her words, though softly spoken, fell with a thud on my heart.

She was serious and I was scared to death. I can't remember exactly how the drama unfolded—it's all a bit of a blur to me now—but I can recall standing in complete shock as she told me that we needed to have "space."

"Space?!" I yelped. "I'll give you all the space you need—just tell me we're still getting married."

"I can't do that," Leslie cried.

I cried too.

"What's this all about?" I pleaded. "I thought everything was good."

"It is good, but I just need to know for sure that I'm making this decision as much as you are," she said.

I could not have been more devastated. More crushed. More heart-broken. Breaking up? Us? How could this be? If I hadn't known it before, I knew it now: love hurts. The route to finding lasting love is tortu-ous. Of course, Leslie and I did get back together and the wedding went on as scheduled. But for the six weeks we were apart, I never felt more alone in my life.

The experience of unrequited love—not just a minor crush, but an intense passionate yearning—is virtually universal at some point in everyone's love life. A study involving more than one-hundred-fifty men and women found that only two percent had never loved someone who spurned them, or found themselves the object of romantic pas-sion they did not reciprocate.

"I think when you first start dating," says comedian Jerry Seinfeld, "they ought to give you three 'Get Out of Relationship Free' cards." If only it were that easy. In this chapter we don't pretend to take the pain out of breaking up, but we do propose a realistic method for breaking up without falling apart. We begin with a quick exploration of why some people stay in a bad relationship. We then help you determine whether or not your relationship deserves a serious break. Much of the chapter is then devoted to specific advice for "heartbreakers" and the "broken-hearted." We provide specific suggestions for initiating and responding to a breakup. We conclude the chapter with a brief synopsis of what you can expect in the aftermath of a dating relationship gone sour.

WHY SOME STAY IN A BAD RELATIONSHIP

The investment of time, energy, and even money can lead some people to hang onto an unhappy relationship in the belief that the pay-off is coming soon. They don't want to have wasted their efforts. They don't want to have "failed." Some may stay in an unhealthy relation-ship because of social pressure. We recently spoke to a seemingly mature woman who had legitimate reasons for breaking up with her boyfriend, but because her friends wanted her to attend a big year-end party with them as a "couple," she was putting off the breakup for a couple months. Another reason some stay in an unsatisfactory relationship is because they don't have an alternative. The ol' plenty-of-fish-in-the-sea maxim rings hollow for them—so they stay stuck.

There are a variety of reasons a person might stay in an unhappy dating relationship, but by far the most common is this: *Even a bad relationship can bring a feeling of security.* No matter how false it actually is, the feeling of being "involved" brings assurance. People in these kinds of relationships usually won't admit it, but like a familiar pair of worn-out shoes, their relationship provides a sense of comfort they can't seem to give up— no matter how bad the relationship really is.

> The best divorce is the one you get before you get married.
>
> —Folk saying

Bruce, a twenty-four-year-old, recently admitted to us that he has been in a dating relationship for nearly two years that is "going nowhere." He told us that hardly a weekend goes by where they don't end up fighting. Their interests are at polar extremes; he likes race cars, she's into novels. They don't even pretend to like what the other is into. More troubling than their divergent interests, however, is their lack of shared values. Bruce is committed to his faith while she wants nothing to do with church. "I don't know why we're still together," he told us. "I guess it's just nice to know there is someone there for me."

Really? It didn't sound like they were there for each other. Was Bruce serious? Indeed he was. Like every other lonely heart in a no-good dating relationship, Bruce's only love was security. The human compulsion for security is stronger than a magnet. It can play serious tricks on our faculties. And since we often don't like the anxiety that comes from making waves, we don't rock the boat. We sit quietly in our relationship, going nowhere, drifting aimlessly when we should be making some tough decisions.

IS IT TIME TO BREAK UP?

"I don't know what to do," Jennifer whined. "I like Greg a lot and we have our fun moments—but something doesn't feel right." Sound familiar? We hear this kind of statement on a regular basis from persons entering the foggy bog of uneasiness about their relationship. Jennifer and Greg had been dating for nearly eight months when she confessed: "I can't tell if it's worth it or not." If you've ever wondered the same thing, we want to help you cut through the nebulous emotions and see your condition more clearly.

There are probably countless reasons why couples split, but in a study that asked more than a hundred-fifty dating couples who had just broken up to write an anonymous essay on "why we broke up," three reasons appeared again and again.[1] *Desire for autonomy* topped the list.

Some men (27 percent) and many women (44 percent) complained of feeling trapped by their dating partner. "He was upset whenever I went out with friends," a typical woman wrote, "even if I couldn't have been with him at that time because of his obligations." Another man said, "I felt like a possession." Most people want intimacy and connection in a dating relationship, but not at the price of reasonable freedom.

> Tis better to have loved and lost than to be stuck with a real loser for the rest of your entire, miserable existence!
>
> —Hallmark coffee mug slogan

Lack of similarity was next on the list of reasons for breaking up. Both men and women discovered that as the relationship progressed, their attitudes, beliefs, values, or interests simply did not jibe. Whether it involved deeply held religious convictions or something as seemingly frivolous as an unmatched sense of humor, lack of similarity was a commonly cited reason for breaking up. If a relationship is "worth it" we need to feel connected, in sync on things that matter to us.

Lack of supportiveness was the third most common reason for a breakup. Many men and women complained that their dates were not encouraging, sympathetic, or understanding. "He's become a jerk," is the way one person put it. "He never listens to what I have to say . . . he's inconsiderate and thoughtless about my feelings . . . he cares more about sports than he does about me." If we don't feel supported by the person we are dating, we want out.

These three common reasons for breaking up may or may not apply to your situation, but if you are still feeling like "something doesn't feel right" about your dating relationship, Exercise 29 in the workbook provides a self-test that can help you uncover some additional reasons you may want to call it quits.

●◆ Exercise 29: Is It Time to Break Up?

It may be time to break up if . . . How would you finish this sentence? If you're not sure, this exercise in the *Relationships Workbook* will help you do so. It will help you know for sure when it's time to break up.

Discovering legitimate reasons for ending a dating relationship is, unfortunately, only the first painful step toward breaking up. The hard part is still to come. And because it is so difficult and because it hurts, it's easy to put it off—like delaying a root canal while the decay continues to fester. Even in a bad relationship it's easy to tell yourself you can work it out. It's easy to limp along and hope it might get better. Truth is that breaking up can be the kindest cruelty. Sure it's going to be painful for both of you, but the best thing you can do for an unhealthy relationship is call it off. A breakup stops a relationship before either of you gets hurt too badly. It allows you to take what was good about what you shared together and leave the bad behind. It frees you both to start over with someone else.

Next, we take a good look at exactly how to do just that. We'll explore what you can do if you are the proactive "heartbreaker" as well as how to respond if you are the one mending a broken heart.

WHEN YOU'RE THE HEARTBREAKER

Every broken heart has a heartbreaker. You may not want to admit it, but it's true. It's also true that some heartbreakers are more graceful than others. But how do you spurn someone gracefully? There's no easy answer. The following suggestions, however, may help you sever the ties to a romance without shattering the other person's heart.

Talk to a Confidant

If the idea of breaking up is rolling around your head, you may be tempted to keep it to yourself. That's not entirely a bad idea, but be careful. While blabbing your plans for an impending breakup is certainly ill advised, talking to someone you trust, someone who cares about you, can help you clarify your thinking. Perhaps you have a brother or sister you can share openly with, or even a parent who can be objective. Then there are your close friends. Very often, nobody commiserates better than a dear ally who has been through a breakup too.

If none of these people do the trick, you might consider talking through your relationship difficulties with a counselor. A professional who listens intently to your every word can bring clarity to your decision so you are confident about what you are doing. A trusted counselor can also help you begin the recovery process in the aftermath of a breakup.

The point is that if your relationship is not going well and if you have even the smallest sense that you may be headed toward a split, you need a confidant for a sounding board. In addition to helping you make your decision, a confidant can also help you determine an appropriate time and place to break up.

Don't Put It Off

Let's face it. If you are like most people you probably have an aversion to endings—even when you desperately want out of a relationship. You probably prefer to take the passive mode, allowing the relationship to somehow end itself. Right? You don't want to be bothered with a dra-

matic farewell, misread motives, and excruciating discussions. So you put it off. You
wait until the tension is so
high your date has to bring it
up. He or she senses a breakup
brewing and tries to get you to

> When one wants to break off, one
> writes to announce the break. When one
> really wants to break off, one doesn't
> write.
>
> —⫚ Simone de Beauviour

'fess up. That's when you act as though you've been served a subpoena
and pretend your date is imagining the whole thing. It's all part of the
breakup game, and you think if you can quit the game without ever talking about it, you can win. But you can't. If you're going to break off a
relationship—and be healthy about it—you've got to work up the nerve
to take action.

"But I never hurt anyone before," you're saying. You may feel
guilty. That's understandable. You're not alone. The inability to tell
another person there's no hope for your relationship is common. Who,
after all, wants to bear bad news? But if you lay low, continue to be
"nice," and wait, hoping the infatuation will fade, you're only making
matters worse. The longer you put it off, the more pain you cause. So
don't enter a conspiracy of silence when it comes to your feelings. Don't
plead the Fifth Amendment. That strategy almost always backfires. It
can feed the fantasy of romance for the other person and inadvertently
encourage him or her to pursue you even more. When it comes to breaking up, the time is now.

Make It a Clean Break

"He just doesn't get it," we hear heartbreakers say. "What do I have
to do, spell it out for him?" Yes! You do. You may think the humane
thing is to hem and haw about the issue, or maybe a gradual series of
disappointments will do the trick. You think that if you make the other
person miserable he or she will break up with you. But that's emotional
terrorism. It whittles down the other person's self-esteem to zero.

The best approach is to be honest and direct. That doesn't mean you say your piece and disappear like the Lone Ranger. But it does mean you send a clear message: *This romantic relationship is over.* The key is to communicate this message in the context of compassion. How do you do this? First of all, you communicate it in person. That may sound obvious, but you might be surprised how many people say "good-bye" on the phone, sometimes through an answering machine. We know of one relationship where the heartbreaker actually had his sister tell his girl-friend the relationship had ended. If you have any decency, you can't break up via an absentee ballot. So to make a clean break, be honest and be present.

Being honest, by the way, is not the same as being brutal. We've known some heartbreakers who are down right mean. Wishing they could close their eyes and make the relationship go away, they lose all sense of common courtesy and point out every frailty the person ever had. On the other end of the heartbreak continuum are those who sug-arcoat the rejection with conciliatory words. They send mixed messages, saying to the unwanted person something like, "I really like our rela-tionship, but it's moving so fast and I just want to enjoy a good friend-ship before we rush into anything." Translation: "I'm not interested in you for a romantic relationship, so it's over." The problem with being so conciliatory is that the other person will never really hear what you want them to hear. They will read into your nice words a lot of hope for your future together. The would-be ex seizes on the positive side of the message and disregards what you intended.

> The fiercest agonies have shortest reign.
>
> —— William Cullen Bryant

If you are going to make a clean break, you can still be gentle. But you've got to be honest. Begin by telling the person what you like and ap-preciate about them. Point out their strengths and what drew you to them in the beginning. Express what you like about your relationship in general. Confess your difficulty in what you are about to tell them and then say it straight out: "I want to break up." Explain your reasons for ending the romance in terms of your own values rather than pointing out what you think is wrong with the other person.

Don't make promises you can't keep. Don't say, for example, that you want to remain good friends when you know that isn't likely. While some couples can break up and remain friends, it's rare. And planting that idea during a breakup can lead the other person, as well as yourself, to expect too much from one another.

•❖ Exercise 30: Making a Clean Break

Are you the kind of person who is able to make a clean break when it is time to break up? Or are you more likely to dance around the issue, hoping the uncomfortable situation will take care of itself? This exercise in the *Relationships Workbook* will help you know where you stand and give you the insight to do what you need to do.

Grieve the Loss

You've done it. You're free. You've severed the chains that bound you to a relationship no longer serving its purpose. Ready for Disneyland? Probably not. A grieving period is required at the end of every romantic relationship, in spite of the fact that you're glad it's over. Yes, *you* initiated the loss, *you* chose it, but it's still traumatic.

Even initiating the end of a terribly bad relationship can be extremely difficult and stressful. Research by Dr. Roy Baumeister at Case Western Reserve University revealed, in fact, that the person who initiates a breakup *can* suffer more unhappiness than the person who is being rejected.[2] Studying the emotional highs and lows in accounts of more than two hundred incidents of unrequited love, Baumeister discovered that unpleasant emotions such as frustration, anger, anxiety, and guilt were mentioned about a third more often in the reports told by the person who ended the relationship. So don't set yourself up to think you'll be ready to celebrate after ending the relationship. Give yourself time, lots of time, to grieve the loss.

WHEN YOU'RE THE BROKENHEARTED

Camped out in bed with a pint of chunky monkey ice-cream and the TV clicker? Thinking about buying a one-way ticket to an obscure Mediterranean island to live the rest of your life as a recluse? Being left by the one you love has a way of making anyone a little loony. If you find yourself on the receiving end of a rejection, however, the following suggestions will help you keep your sanity.

Face Reality

Dumped by her boyfriend-the-doctor, Marie was deep in denial. She became obsessed with the idea of winning him back. Convinced that their relationship had ended because she hadn't taken enough interest in his work, Marie spent nights in the local library, poring over medical journals and developing a morbid fascination with the inner workings of the human body. She kept photos of her ex all over her apartment. Her friends were embarrassed and tried to help by telling her that taking Anatomy 101 was not going to win him back. Yet for months Marie went on as though the relationship was only going through temporary trouble. But it wasn't. The relationship was permanently over and Marie couldn't admit it.

Marie is fairly typical. Getting "dumped" is difficult to accept. The notion of getting together again is a familiar one among the jilted. Some part of our soul is convinced that the other person feels the same way we do, only they don't know it yet.

> To love and win is the best thing; to love and lose the next best.
>
> —W. Thackeray

All of us have a hard time coming to terms with rejection. Interestingly, men are more likely than women to deny the end of a romance— by a ratio of three to two.[3] Part of the reason for this is that men are prone to romantic crushes on women who are far more desirable than themselves and so find their love more frequently unrequited. Whatever your gender, however, you've got to face reality. You've got to admit the relationship is over and move on. Why? Because the price you pay for denial is your dignity. People who won't admit it's over sacrifice their self-respect. They substitute desperation for dignity, and that's never a pretty picture.

Let Yourself Cry

Okay, okay. You ski the black diamond slopes, walk barefoot on hot asphalt, skydive for fun, so what's a little romantic split? Truth is, a breakup is one of the toughest things you'll ever experience. It's heartwrenching, and you deserve to feel lousy. Breaking up from even an unhealthy relationship hurts. It's frightening to lose a relationship you depended on. So give yourself over to the agony and have a good cry. You'll feel better. Scientific studies have shown that tears actually excrete certain depression-purging hormones so that you begin to feel better physically and emotionally after a good cry. It literally cleanses the soul. So express your sadness instead of keeping it in, and the healing will begin all the sooner.

Perhaps you don't need any encouragement in this department, but if you do, we have a suggestion. Tune in any pop radio station and you'll hear dozens of breakup tunes, one after the other. Why? Because music helps us express emotions that aren't always easy to articulate. Music is a means to catharsis. Whether you're alone on a Friday night or driving in your car to run a few errands, give yourself permission to bawl like a baby.

> To have known love, how bitter a thing it is.
>
> —Algernon Charles Swinburne

One note of caution: If you are depressed and still crying several months after the breakup, you may need help from a trained professional. How do you know? The following symptoms may indicate a more severe form of depression than is typical after grieving the loss of a love: trouble sleeping, loss of appetite or excessive eating, social withdrawal, pessimism, and thoughts of harming yourself. Don't worry, by the way, that you will bring these symptoms on by allowing yourself to cry after your breakup; the very opposite is more likely.

Stop Blaming Yourself

"I guess I'm one of those people who's meant to be alone," admits twenty-four-year-old Sarah, a normally upbeat assistant manager of a local clothing store who was recently dumped by her boyfriend. "My track record is awful when it comes to picking men, and I need to concentrate on work if I'm going to be able to take care of myself in the future." Her latest dating disaster was the result of a five-month relationship that ended when he cheated on Sarah with one of her friends. "I feel like an idiot for having been so gullible," she says. "I don't trust men—or my own judgment—and I deserve to be by myself forever."

Sarah, like many brokenhearted people, had lost faith in herself. It's one of the saddest things we hear in our relationship counseling, and we've come to believe a lot of this self-blame is the result of self-help formulas that tell us we must be stupid to have chosen a person who later does us wrong. Yes, you do have to take a hard look at your own behavior if you always make bad relationship choices, but why punish yourself because you fell in love? Self-blame will do nothing to help you learn from mistakes and become a better person.

People who have been burned too often take the blame. They feel guilty for failing at yet "another" relationship. Eventually, they end up converting their guilt into an unhealthy compulsion: overeating, abusing drugs or alcohol, sexual trysts with near strangers, and avoidance of intimacy altogether. Don't get caught in the guilt trap. You aren't so powerful that you can cause someone else's behavior. You can play a part in it, but you can't *cause* it. You are not to blame.

•◆ Exercise 31: Avoiding the Blame Game

Do you have a difficult time buying the idea that you are not to blame for your breakup? Do you feel totally responsible? Do you think that you could have somehow prevented it from happening? If so, you will want to take a moment to complete this exercise in the *Relationships Workbook*. It will help you get a clearer picture of just how hard you are being on yourself.

Steer Clear of Revenge

"I feel like roadkill on the highway of love," said Justin as he sat in our office, "and I ain't gonna be that for nobody." His face was red, his teeth were clenched, and the veins in his forehead were protruding. "I'm gonna get even with Jenny if it's the last thing I do!"

Yikes! We never saw Justin again after this angry speech and don't know if he ever "got

> Heaven has no rage like love to hatred turned.
>
> —*William Congreve*

even" with his ex-girlfriend, but he's not the only one we've heard talk this way. Sometimes a breakup experience is so ugly, so nasty, the antidote seems to lie in revenge. We know of a woman who was so angry with the man who dumped her that she decided to blast him by starting a string of vicious rumors—everything from his having a third-grade dependence on his mother to his problem with being a sociopathic liar. Hell hath no fury like a man or woman told to hit the road.

If the getting-even scenario seems to fit the bill for your situation, however, beware: revenge will eat you alive. "Something of vengeance I had tasted for the first time," wrote English novelist Charlotte Brontë in *Jane Eyre*, "as aromatic wine it seemed, on swallowing, warm and racy: its after-flavour, metallic and corroding, gave me a sensation as if I had been poisoned." Our advice is to learn from Brontë's insight. Don't get even. Get over it. You'll be the better and stronger person for doing so.

Beware of Rebounding

Feeling rejected by the person you care about is enough to drive almost anyone into the arms of the first willing person who comes along after the breakup. The experience, in fact, is so common it has a name: rebounding. But don't allow yourself to fall into this trap. If you do, chances are you're only setting yourself up for another heartache. Why? Research shows that people on the rebound tend to fall in love with people who will soon reject them.[4]

Most vulnerable to this kind of rejection are men and women who are so anxious about being loved that they drive their partners away through being too clingy. So afraid of being abandoned, they glom onto almost anyone who will have them. They lose all sensible perspective and don't see the new person as he or she really is. We've seen it dozens of times and it's always sad. The desperate, brokenhearted person trades in their critical judgment for the off chance that this new person will love them like no other. And what do you know? They do. They love them like no other person in particular—just another bottom feeder in the food chain of love that is looking for vulnerable prey. Don't let it be you.

WHAT TO EXPECT AFTER BREAKING UP

Bouncing back from a breakup is never easy. Not surprisingly, however, it is usually easier to leave someone than to be left. Research clearly shows that both men and women feel considerably less depressed, less lonely, and more relieved when they were the heartbreaker than when they are the brokenhearted. In fact the emotional reactions of partners tends to be almost the mirror opposite of one another: the happier one person is to get out, the worse the other feels about the breakup.

It is fair to say, however, that breaking off a relationship, even a bad one, is never free from pain for either person.[5] Married couples who fought constantly are often surprised to discover, once separated, how emotionally attached they remain to each other. The same is seen in children who persist in their attachment to a cold or abusive parent long after the parent has abandoned them.[6] Whether you are the breaker or the breakee, you can expect to suffer loss. You can expect to grieve.

Contrary to stereotypes, by the way, studies suggest that men suffer over a breakup at least as much as women do.[7] In fact, in one study men reported longer-lasting grief after breaking up than the women did.[8] Also, a number of studies find that for women, the worst time emotionally is before the breakup, whereas for men it is after the breakup.[9] Why is this? One reason is that women initiate breakups more than men do and thus feel in more control of the situation.[10] Another reason is that women have more friends to help them deal with their distress after the breakup. Women also tend to be better prepared for their losses because they are more aware of their emotional dependency in a relationship. Men, on the other hand, often do not invest much time or energy in thinking about their relationship until it has fallen apart.[11] As a result, they may not be aware of how dependent they have become on a partner for emotional support—and be traumatized when they are far more upset than they expected to be.

> We are never so defenseless against suffering as when we love, never so helplessly unhappy as when we have lost our loved object or its love.
>
> —Sigmund Freud

Whether you are male or female, the breaker or the breakee, you can expect to experience some fairly predictable phases of grief following the dissolution of any romantic relationship. No one has done more to help us understand the experience of grief than pioneering researcher Elisabeth Kübler-Ross.[12] While her studies of over two hundred terminally ill patients focused on physical death, they can also shed light on the death of love. Her five phases include: denial, anger, bargaining, depression, and acceptance. Admittedly, these phases are not clear-cut, and any person may move back and forth between any two of them. Grief is never smooth. Let's take a closer look at each one.

The first phase for many after a breakup is *denial*. This numbing effect is especially common for the people being rejected who don't see it coming. Without warning, they are dropped like the proverbial hot potato and are in a state of shock. "This can't be happening," they say to themselves. "This isn't real." How can someone be so fully present in your life one moment and gone the next? How can the delight and affection you shared together suddenly disappear like a rabbit in a cheap magician's act? In this initial stage of denial, the collapse of the relationship seems incomprehensible.

With time (sometimes a few minutes, sometimes a few days), however, numbing fades and gives way to the next phase—*anger*. After the reality of a breakup has sunk in, there is a nasty little imp that emerges in nearly all of us that wants to get mad, if not even. We recently talked to a young woman on the campus where we teach who attempted suicide to scare her ex-boyfriend after he broke up with her. "I didn't really want to die," she confessed, "I just wanted him to know that he can't throw me away and expect it to be okay." Another angry ploy that is far more common than this woman's angry tactic is the you-didn't-breakup-with-*me-I*-broke-up-with-you game. By reversing the roles (if only in self-perception), the breakee feels more powerful, more in control. Of course, the heartbreaker can also experience this anger phase. It is usually exhibited in recounting all the terrible things the other person did to deserve being rejected.

After the anger subsides, *bargaining* enters the picture. In this phase, the brokenhearted and sometimes the heartbreakers yearn for another chance to revive their dying relationship. "I can be different" becomes the theme song of the rejected. "Maybe I should give him another chance" becomes the anthem of the rejecter. In both cases, these people barter with guilt and self-loathing while scheming (if only internally) to keep the relationship on life support. Not willing to let go of the little ember of hope they still have for their love life, they desperately search for anything that might keep the relationship going. They try frantically to fan the flame and keep it burning. Sometimes these desperate efforts succeed for a while, but they usually end up only prolonging the inevitable breakup.

Once you have tried to negotiate your way back into a relationship and failed at that too, *depression* is the natural next phase. So you check into heartbreak hotel, pull the blinds, unplug the phone, and listen to every song ever written about the aftermath of breaking up: "Unbreak My Heart," "Love on the Rocks," "All By Myself," every radio station's play list seems custom selected just for you. So you recall fond memories that sometimes stab you with pain, and you sulk in sadness. All alone. But that's okay. In fact, it's healthy. You deserve to feel depressed after losing someone you love. John Bowlby, the English psychiatrist whose studies of bereavement and grief are fundamental, states in his book *Loss* that "sadness is a normal and healthy response to any misfortune."[13] He goes on to say that without experiencing depression after this kind of loss we will suffer all the more later on. This phase allows us to cry out our pain and wash our souls of toxic feelings. Perhaps the most important thing to remember about sadness and depression is that they almost always diminish with the passage of time. And when they do, you enter the final phase—*acceptance*.

Acceptance, according to poet Robert Frost, comes when we bow to the end of a love, when we recognize its season has passed. Once we have adjusted to the initial jolt and resolved our reflexive anger, once we have given up bargaining and healed our hurting hearts, acceptance takes care of the rest by relinquishing the relationship to its natural course. No more coercion. No more game playing. No more false expectations. No more pain. Only acceptance. "When I was breaking up with Karen," a young man recently told us, "I thought my heart was literally going to break in two. I was upset and couldn't eat for days. I eventually got deeply depressed." He told us it had now been nearly nine months since his girlfriend initiated the split. "No one could have convinced me I would ever get over Karen," he said, "but in time I did." He went on to tell us how he and Karen rarely if ever talk these days, but that he is grateful for having known her and that he learned "tons" from their relationship. That's the mark of acceptance. You know you've come to a place of acceptance when you have shored up your self-regard, learned a few lessons, and have the strength to go on.

◆ Exercise 32: Moving On

Knowing what you have and haven't experienced in relation to the phases of grief and loss can help you move through them more effectively. This exercise in the *Relationships Workbook* will help you assess where you stand in the process of recovering and get you to a place where you can move on.

If you have journeyed through these phases following a breakup, you know that they are not simple and straightforward. Some overlap and coexist. Others may be skipped altogether. Whatever the path, however, the destination remains the same: acceptance. Does this mean that you and your ex become "just friends"? Hardly.

So how often are men and women able to remain friends after a breakup? It depends. If both you and your partner agreed to split, your chances of remaining friends increase. But few breakups are truly mutual. Research shows fifty-one percent of breakups are initiated by the woman and forty-two percent by the man. This means that only seven percent are truly mutual. Interestingly, if the man breaks up with the woman it is far more likely to become a friendly relationship. If the woman initiates the breakup with the man, remaining "just friends" rarely happens.

FOR REFLECTION

- What have you learned from watching others go through breakups? What have you witnessed that seemed to make sense, and what would you say would be good to avoid?
- Can you think of a time when you stayed in an unhappy relationship (of any kind) because of the security it provided? What allowed you to finally move on?

- As the initiator of a breakup, what would you do to make the split less painful for the person you are leaving?
- As the person on the receiving end of a breakup, what would you personally do to keep your self-esteem intact?
- Of all the phases one can expect to experience after a breakup (denial, anger, bargaining, depression, and acceptance), which one do you think is most important and why?

chapter nine

Relating to God Without Feeling Phony

*My soul thirsts for God, for the living God.
When can I go and meet with God?*

—⌇ Psalm 42:2

A reporter once asked the great theologian Karl Barth: "Sir, you have written many huge volumes about God; how do you know it is all true?" The learned German scholar is said to have responded, "My mother told me."

I (Les) know just what he meant. I was brought up in a religious home—a parsonage, no less—and I make no bones about it. I inherited my faith in God about the time I was old enough to eat graham crackers. And looking back, it's quite remarkable that the faith which held me so early in life is still with me.

Or is it?

As a child, I didn't weigh the evidence for accepting or rejecting religious beliefs. In fact, I didn't even know there were options. As I entered the awkward age of middle adolescence, I had a thousand doubts about myself, but my faith held strong. It survived peer pressure and a certain amount of rebellion. The memorized lines from Vacation Bible

School took on meaning and I could often quote them on cue. My faith was fully defended and nothing could shake it. Well, almost nothing.

In college I learned to evaluate and question. My professors asked me to test and critique everything from Elizabethan poetry to the laws of physics. I was encouraged to question presuppositions in almost every field. So it was inevitable that I eventually evaluate my inherited faith and memorized answers. I remember when it began. As a college sophomore, sitting in the cafeteria, I suddenly saw my routine of saying the blessing at meals in a new light. The whole thing seemed perfunctory, a meaningless ritual, an unexamined but persistent—even compulsive—act. I wondered why I prayed. Was it because I was thankful, or did I just want to appear thankful? Was it because I knew God, or did I want to appear as though I knew God? I didn't know. Suddenly I was swimming in an ocean of doubt.

The behaviors I was taught as a child seemed superficially related to my beliefs. Prayer, going to church, reading Scripture, giving to the needy, Bible study groups, mission trips—all seemed vain. Each was like a stone in my pocket, making it more and more difficult to stay afloat.

> Doubt is a pain too lonely to know that faith is his twin brother.
>
> —⅃ Kahlil Gibran

Before being entirely submersed I owned up to my desperate doubt and found myself holding the heaviest stone yet, guilt. On top of the agony of doubt, I was faced with this Goliath of an emotion. I felt ashamed for doubting what seemed to be so meaningful to others, and I felt guilty for not accepting their answers. The problem was that their answers, though meant to be a lifeline, felt more like an anchor.

It wasn't "unbelief" or stubborn resistance. This was doubt—the honest admission that in spite of all the answers, rather significant questions are still outstanding. My once articulate prayers dwindled down to a single word: "Why?" This desperate question was sprayed like chemical foam on the fire of my heart. I asked the question again and again. Why? Why? God was silent.

I'm not sure how long I suffered in the darkness of doubt—perhaps six months or more—but somewhere in the midst of my lonely questioning I realized something that eventually revolutionized my faith: I was not searching for an explanation. I was longing for a relationship.

This chapter explores the relationship we all long to ultimately experience. It's about finding and meeting God. It's about starting and nurturing an honest relationship with our Creator. It's about coming to terms with ourselves in connection with a sometimes mystical deity. This is not a chapter about how God can be your buddy. Such trivialization makes a mockery of this divine connection. Here you will discover who God is and why we desperately need a relationship with him. Steering clear of religious jargon and platitudes, we'll also explore how mere mortals like you and me can enjoy an authentic and meaningful relationship with the Almighty. We begin this quest with the most obvious issue: how to find God when he feels distant.

FINDING GOD

Elie Wiesel, a survivor of the Nazi death camps, tells of a Rabbi he knew at Auschwitz. "He used to pray all the time, . . . he would recite whole passages of the Talmud from memory . . . and one day he said to me: 'It's the end. God is no longer with us.'" Wiesel goes on to say that the Rabbi quickly added these words in a faint voice:

"I know. One has no right to say things like that. I know. . . . But what can I do? I'm not a sage, one of the elect, nor a saint. I'm just an ordi-

> If God lived on earth, people would break his windows.
>
> —↯ Jewish Proverb

nary creature of flesh and blood. I've got eyes, too, and I can see what they are doing here. Where is the divine Mercy? Where is God? How can I believe, how could anyone believe, in this Merciful God?"[1]

It doesn't take a Nazi concentration camp to provoke such soul-searching questions. All of us—with various amounts of suffering—have wondered where God is. My life's suffering could never even begin to compare with anyone who experienced Auschwitz, but my doubt in God was just as real. I too was asking, *Where is God?*

In the midst of my spiritual struggle, a well-meaning pastor told me that "an atheist does not find God for the same reason a thief does not find a policeman. He is not looking for him." But I *was* looking for God. I believed. I was crying out to God. And yet there was no answer. Day after day, my faith began to fade until I was on the brink of giving up.

That's when something happened. I can almost point to the spot. I was driving to Chicago's O'Hare airport. Dad was arriving from a business trip, and I was happy to pick him up. When I was small, Dad would almost always return from an adventure with a small gift—a model airplane from Washington D.C., a miniature orange crate from Los Angeles, a baseball cap from Boston. The excitement of knowing that Dad would pull a small package from his briefcase was enough to send me into orbit. That was long ago. On this trip I didn't expect a memento.

As I drove past the stubbled fields of February farmland I resisted the urge to turn on the radio. I used the opportunity to spend a few minutes with the One I doubted. That's not as strange as it sounds. Most of the time I didn't really doubt God's existence—or even religious doctrines. I did question the Bible, God's sovereignty, the Resurrection, and miracles. But mostly I doubted my heart. I questioned the motives behind my behavior.

My prayer, like the hundreds before, continued to be filled with questions: "Why do I feel so empty? Why do you feel so distant? Sometimes I feel like I am a robot just going through the motions. It seems I'm more concerned with doing things right than I am with doing the right things. God, why are you so silent?"

Mingled among fond memories and softly spoken prayers, my faith began to reappear. As I drove along Interstate 55 there was no miraculous sign. No message written in the sky. I simply found myself anticipating Dad's arrival and humming a familiar hymn: "It is well with my soul."

And it *was* well. Doubt was quick to submerge the meaning of my faith. But in a strange paradox, it was my honest questioning that was now allowing me to grasp God's hand and be pulled from the water. And when I did, he was there not with a lifeline or a life jacket, but as a living lifeguard. That's when I realized I didn't need answers; I wanted a relationship. Just as I didn't need gifts upon my father's return, I didn't need answers from God. I needed to *be* with God.

Now I think I understand God's silence. It was the opportunity to view faith as more than an intellectual "Amen" at the end of a religious proposition. The times I spent with God—like driving to the airport—gave me the space to see that faith is not so much *believing* in God, as it is *being* with God.

Doubt dismantled the faith of my childhood. And I thank God for doubt. It gave me faith—a faith of my own. I have come to understand what Tennyson meant when he said, "There lies more faith in honest doubt than in all your creeds."

> The time came when the beliefs in which I was once brought up and which, in fact, had given my life direction even while my intellect still challenged their validity, were recognized by me as mine in their own right and by my free choice.
>
> —Dag Hammarskjöld

Too often in our relationship with God, we expect continuous certainty promoted by intellectual innocence. We feel uneasy with, or even resent, a believer who doubts. We lose sight of the fact that faith matures because of, not in spite of, doubt. We forget that if a question is not seriously asked, one will miss the richness and depth of the answer. In fact the most destructive thing we can do to our relationship with God when it is passing through a period of honest uncertainty is to silence our doubts and repress our questions. "Repressed doubts have a high rate of resurrection," according to John Powell, "and doubts that are plowed under will only grow new roots."

If you want to relate to God without feeling phony, therefore, you've got to 'fess up. You've got to admit your doubts, ask your questions, and start getting real with God.

•◊ Exercise 33: Honest-to-Goodness Doubt

What is your experience of doubt? Does it impact your relationship with God? Does your doubt go buried in an attempt to pretend that everything about your faith is fine? This exercise in the *Relationships Workbook* will help you face your doubts head on in an attempt to build a stronger faith.

WHO IS GOD?

According to a contemporary parable, a group of scientists were recently commissioned to build a computer which could answer with scientific precision the question of God's existence. After completing the most intricate, sophisticated computer ever assembled, the scientists carefully fed the question into their machine: "Is there a God?" After several minutes of humming and whirring, the answer came out. It read: "There is *now*."

> You know you're finding God when you believe that God is good—no matter what happens.
>
> —↯ Larry Crabb

Like these scientists, the God we know is often the God we create. Sigmund Freud, founder of modern psychology, proposed that God is nothing more than the imaginary projection of the father figure.[2] In other words, we use our imagination to create a god that makes sense to us. As children, we look to our fathers to supply our needs, to protect us, and to answer our questions. When we reach adulthood, we still long for the comfort and security of a father figure who will be whatever we need. This perpetuation of a father figure, according to Freud, is the basis for all religion and summarily explains away the existence of God.

Emile Durkheim, one of the founders of modern sociology, viewed God as nothing more than a symbolic representation of the collective values of society.[3] In other words, our image of God is characterized by traits people around us prize the most. If we are members of an Anglo-

Saxon, Protestant Republican group that promotes capitalism, God becomes an Anglo-Saxon Protestant Republican just like us. If we are Asian or African-American, God takes on a different set of traits and values that are more closely aligned with our group. So religion, according to Durkheim, is nothing more than a process whereby a group ends up worshiping itself.

Now, you may be thinking that both Freud and Durkheim make pretty good arguments against the existence of God. You may view them as devastating attacks on religion. But if you take their thinking a bit further you will discover that both of them actually underscore the biblical admonitions against making graven images of God.[4] Freud, after all, does not explain away God's existence. His theory of projection simply explains how we conceptualize God. Likewise, Durkheim does not disprove the existence of God; he explains how God is too often created in the image of society.

What do you think? Rather than viewing Freud and Durkheim's theories as negating the possibility of believing in a transcendent, eternal God, do they not simply explain the origin of false deities against which we must struggle? Consider the following distorted concepts of God.

The Referee God

Some people see God as a referee who tallies points for good performance on a huge scoreboard in the sky. These people are consumed by religious rules and the fear that they will step out of line and suffer a penalty. They may get away with a few fouls or errors when God isn't looking, but most of the time these poor people are motivated by guilt and obsessed with avoiding God's wrath. In the game of justice they play, the ref shows no mercy. So they do what they can to rack up points and avoid the whistle.

> Most Christians have enough religion to feel guilty about their sins, but not enough to enjoy life in the Spirit.
>
> —Martin Luther

The Grandfather God

Many people use their interpretation of God to keep them from growing up—to avoid responsibility. And by viewing God as a warm grandfatherly figure, they remain a child. They want to be told, "There's nothing to worry about; I'll take care of everything for you." There is a part of all of us that wants somebody else to step in and do all the hard things we are supposed to do, relieving us of responsibility. A medieval Spanish monk wrote in his journal, "I am confident that, after my death, I will go to heaven because I have never made a decision on my own. I have always followed the orders of superiors, and if ever I erred, the sin is theirs, not mine." The Grandfather-God image conveniently lets us off the hook.

The Scientist God

"A superior reasoning power," is how Einstein conceptualized God. "A superior mind," is how he said it on another occasion. For some, God is a withdrawn and distant thinker, too busy running the galaxies to get involved in our petty problems. God is sitting in his laboratory, conducting experiments with his door closed and a "Do Not Disturb" sign on it. God, from this vantage point, is merely observing human beings as they spin through space on the tiny blue ball called Earth. We are but a kind of cosmic experiment to entertain our Creator.

The Bodyguard God

Some people think of God much the same way a sailor thinks of a lifeboat. He knows it is there, but he hopes he'll never have to use it. These people live life without giving much conscious attention to God, but they expect him to be there when they need him. When we view God this way, we believe he should serve as a kind of bodyguard to protect us from pain and suffering. "If I'm living a good life," so the reasoning goes, "then God should look after me and keep me out of harm's way." Because they are decent human beings, these people believe God should make them immune to illness or injustice. And when he doesn't, God is to blame.

●◆ *Exercise 34: Will the Real God Please Stand Up?*

If you take the time to consider how you sometimes distort God's character, you will come closer to understanding who God really is. This exercise in the *Relationships Workbook* will help you examine how you may be misperceiving God, and it will challenge you to consider one of the most difficult questions you may ever ponder.

A list of distorted images of God could go on and on. God is not a form of Santa Claus, nor a state trooper, nor a sentimental pushover. God is not even a loving parent. God is much more. No human analogy can fully encompass and accurately convey who God is. That's why Freud and Durkheim's theories are unintentionally helpful to anyone wanting an honest-to-goodness relationship with God. Here's the point: Whereas the Bible teaches that human beings are created in the image of God, these social scientists suggest that God is created in our own image. And they are right. That's why if we are going to relate to God without feeling phony, we must first and foremost have an accurate understanding—free from personal distortion—of who God is.

Countless volumes over the centuries have been written by philosophers and theologians on the attributes of God. And we are not so naive as to think we can sum up God's character in a few paragraphs of this chapter. So permit us to lift out of Scripture God's cardinal trait, the one quality that describes who God is more than any other: *God is Love.*

One of the most quoted verses in all of Scripture underscores this truth: "For God so loved the world that he gave his one and only Son. . . ."[5] God does not just give love, however; God *is* love. In Camus' novel *The Plague*, the priest Paneloux tells his congregation repeatedly that the outbreak of bubonic plague in their city is God's judgment on them for their sins and that ultimately God works all things for the best. When an innocent child dies in agony shortly thereafter, Father Paneloux himself falls ill and dies almost immediately afterward, not so

> Love is pressing around us on all sides like air. Cease to resist, and instantly love takes possession.
>
> —Amy Carmichael

much from the plague, one suspects, as from the experience of having the principles to which he had devoted his whole life proven false. Without that support, how could he live? His God had failed him. His God had no love.

Seeing God in the absence of love is the number one obstacle to building an authentic relationship with him. Love, after all, is God's very essence. Scripture makes this plain: "God is love. Whoever lives in love lives in God, and God in him."[6]

Consider the sun as an analogy. The sun only shines, just as God only loves. It is the nature of the sun to shine, to offer warmth and light. And it is the nature of God to love. We are free to get away from the sun, we can lock ourselves in a dark room, but we do not keep the sun from shining just because we put ourselves in a place where it cannot reach us. So it is with God's love. We can reject it, but God keeps on loving us. No matter what our choices, God still loves. And because God loves us, a relationship with God is possible.

●◆ Exercise 35: Does God Really Love Me?

Everyone struggles at one time or another with this important question: *Does God's grace really include me?* This exercise in the *Relationships Workbook* provides a self-test that will help you determine the degree to which you believe God really does love you.

WHO NEEDS GOD?

In *The City of God*, Augustine expressed a universal human feeling when he said, "O Lord, thou hast made us for thyself, and we are restless until we find our rest in thee." Without an authentic relationship with God, we are left empty and detached. There is in all of us, at the very center of our lives, an aching, a burning in the heart that is deep and insatiable. Most often we try to quench that yearning with a human relationship. We try to fill the gap in our existence with a friend or lover. But no human relationship—no matter how wonderful—can ever complete us.

In the first chapter of this book we explored the "compulsion for completion" that every person brings to an important relationship. And we discovered that this compulsion can never be fulfilled at the human level. It is too much to expect from another person. We may enjoy moments of heart-to-heart connection and even ecstasy with another human being, but these feelings of completion are just that—*feelings*. And feelings are always fleeting. The wholeness we long for in human contact is forever elusive. Why? Because human beings can never make us whole. In short, that's why we need God's love. Only God ultimately satisfies our compulsion

> The infinite abyss can only be filled by an infinite and immutable object, that is, by God himself.
>
> —⳥ Blaise Pascal

for completion. A permanent sense of wholeness is found exclusively in an authentic relationship with God. Every human relationship is but a mere shadow of this one.

What's more, in the absence of an authentic relationship with God we will always come up empty in every other relationship. It is God who satisfies our ultimate longing for belonging and gives us meaning in our lives. It is God who helps us rise above selfishness to take care of others. It is God who fulfills our deepest needs when the one person on earth we were counting on—a friend or a family member—lets us down. And it is God who empowers us to keep moving forward in a relationship that needs help and healing.

How does God satisfy our longing for belonging? How does God help us rise above self-centeredness? The answer is found in who God is. Remember? God is love. And here is a relational principle that is more powerful than dynamite: *We cannot love until we first experience love.* This is why parents need to bathe their little ones in acceptance, affirmation, care, and kindness. The more love we experience in our critical early years, the more mature and healthy our love for others will be as adults. It's a universal tenet. And it's grounded in our innate need for God.

> There are two kinds of people: those who say to God, "thy will be done," and those to whom God says, "All right, then, have it your way."
>
> —A. C. S. Lewis

Love is not something we conjure up through effort, positive thinking, or even prayer. Love is a response to being loved. As Scripture says, "We love because God first loved us."[7] We don't love because we should or because we are instructed to, but because we are loved. Most of us are used to looking at love as a duty. We don't give much thought to being loved by God as the means to loving others. How many sermons have you heard on the virtue of being loved?

Dietrich Bonhoeffer, in his *Ethics*, suggests that in trying to understand that God is love, we must not take the word *love* as our starting point, but we must begin with the word *God*. As the apostle John says, only the person who knows God can know what love really is. "It is not," Bonhoeffer adds, "that we first of all by nature know what love is and therefore know also what God is." In other words, no one can know what love really means unless he or she first knows God through the experience of faith.

So, who needs God? All of us. Not because God's love demands change; but because it produces change. We'll never find what we're looking for in human relationships until we first find a transforming and authentic relationship with God.

●● Exercise 36: Really Relating to God

This exercise in the *Relationships Workbook* will help you get serious about your present relationship with God. It will help you consider what has brought you to where you are in this relationship, and it will help you chart a course to where you would like to be.

HOW DO YOU RELATE TO GOD?

Most people relate to God through their "religion." It's interesting to note, however, that the Bible never uses the word *religion*. The phrase closest in meaning to it is "the fear of God"—a phrase too often misunderstood by even sincere believers. What do these words "the fear of God" mean to you? Do they conjure up the picture of an all-powerful authority living in heaven and thundering his will down on us, ready to smite us if we disobey? Do they make you think of a God who knows your every secret thought and deed, and will punish you if you do wrong? If so, then you are like a lot of people today and throughout the ages whose understanding of religion has been based on fear of punishment. Religion becomes a matter of God's commanding and our obeying and being rewarded, or else disobeying and being punished.

People with this view live in fear of losing God's love. They scurry around doing good deeds and then say, "Now God will see how good and devoted I am, and maybe he will finally love me." I recently worked with a young man who couldn't watch a television commercial without worrying that he was having lustful thoughts about the beautiful model in the ad. I also have a friend who fears she is guilty of sinful pride anytime someone compliments her. Whether victims of self-imposed standards or bad religion, people like this, perpetually afraid of God, are terribly misguided.

The fear of God may indeed be the beginning of wisdom and the cornerstone of proper living, as the Bible repeatedly states. But "the fear

> Love of God is pure when joy and suffering inspire an equal degree of gratitude.
>
> —⊥ Simone Weil

of God" does not mean being afraid of God. "The fear of God" is not fear as we use the word today, but *awe* and *reverence*. Fear is a negative emotion. It is constricting. It makes us want to run away from whatever we are afraid of. It makes us feel angry and resentful. Awe and reverence, on the other hand, is the experience of being overwhelmed, of confronting someone or something much more powerful than ourselves.

Awe is a positive feeling, an expansive feeling. Where fear makes us want to run away, awe makes us want to draw closer even as we hesitate to get too close. Instead of resenting our own smallness or weakness, we stand in appreciation of something greater than ourselves. And we want to linger.

The point is that if you are going to build an authentic relationship with God, you cannot do so through blind submission, repressing every doubt. And you cannot do so out of guilt and fear. God is not impressed by your groveling.

Let's cut to it. If you want to relate to God without feeling phony, you've got to get rid of everything that distorts, dilutes, or compromises the person you were meant to be, until only your authentic self— created in God's image—remains. The bottom line? You've got to get real. Be honest. You've got to take off any sanctimonious mask you may be wearing and be angry, depressed, excited, or anything else you consider "bad" before God. The more you can admit who you are—even when you wish you were different—the deeper your relationship with God will grow.

Once you come to God as a real person, you are ready to build a relationship like any other. *But God is invisible*, you say, *and mysterious.* True. But God also provided us with a flesh-and-blood connection to himself through Jesus Christ. Two thousand years ago a baby, "the Son of God,"[8] was born in Bethlehem and lived an earthly life. In Christ, God took the form of a human and lived, not as a celebrity with bodyguards or even as royalty surrounded by special treatment, but as an ordinary person born to the Virgin Mary. In human flesh, Jesus experienced a range of emotions: playfulness with children, sympathy for the sick, joy with his disciples, anger at legalists, grief for the brokenhearted, loneliness and anguish in Gethsemane and on the cross. Jesus was God in human form. So when you consider how you might relate to an "invisible" God without feeling phony, consider how you might relate to Jesus. Not the Jesus surrounded by cultural clichés or the Sunday school figure on a flannelgraph board. But the brilliant, creative, chal-

lenging, fearless, compassionate, unpredictable, and ultimately loving Jesus who will
stretch your faith and bring
you closer to God than you
ever imagined.

> No eye has seen, no ear has heard, no mind has conceived what God has prepared for those who love him.
>
> — 1 Corinthians 2:9

But be forewarned: "No one who meets Jesus ever stays the same."
So writes Philip Yancey in his wonderful book *The Jesus I Never Knew*.
As a respected journalist, Philip studied the life of Christ from every
angle—from the manger in Bethlehem to the cross in Jerusalem—and
found a Jesus who wants to radically transform your life.

The transformation, however, only happens through a personal
encounter. Not the kind that hits you out of the blue when you least
expect it. Few people are knocked off their horses, as the apostle Paul
was. No. Most of us encounter Christ when we *make a decision* to know
him. When we set aside time to discover who he is, we begin to form
an honest relationship.

Mark, a friend of ours, travels once a year to the Arizona desert
for a meeting with God. As a busy attorney, he sets aside a full week
each spring to visit a monastery where the monks include him in their
daily routine. Each morning Mark is assigned a mundane chore to complete before breakfast. Around noon he attends a simple worship service, followed by meaningful discussion with a spiritual mentor. At
night Mark sits alone in relative silence, reading, thinking, writing, and
talking with God. Ask him why he does this and he will tell you that
it recharges his spiritual batteries and brings him closer to Christ. But
Mark will quickly add that this intensive time of spiritual renewal is no
substitute for spending time with God in more minor and mundane
moments. He makes a good point. Have you ever put off talking with
a friend until you had more time to "really talk" and then eventually
found that you nearly lost touch with your friend altogether because
you didn't take advantage of what little time you did have? Every relationship requires conscious effort. And in relating to God, that means
turning our hearts and minds to him even in the midst of our busy

and hectic days. It means making God a conscious part of each of our lives—not just at Easter and Christmas, not just on Sundays—but every day.

In his classic novel *One Hundred Years of Solitude*, Colombian author Gabriel García Márquez tells of a village where people are afflicted with a strange plague of forgetfulness, a kind of contagious amnesia. The plague causes people to forget the names of even the most common everyday objects. One young man, still unaffected, tries to limit the damage by putting labels on everything. "This is a table," "This is a window," "This is a cow; it has to be milked every morning." And at the entrance to the town, on the main road, he puts up two large signs. One reads, "The name of our village is Macondo," and the larger one reads, "God exists."

We will all forget much of what we have learned in life. In fact, you may have already forgotten the principles you learned in this book about your family of origin, gender differences, friendships, and love. That's okay. Much of our forgetting will do us relatively little harm. But if we forget to whom we belong, if we forget that our deepest longing is belonging to God, our compulsion for completion drives us into unhealthy relationships. Without God, selfishness pervades our souls and we are truly alone in an unhallowed world. In a God-aware relationship, however, our souls are ultimately satisfied in a meaningful life of goodness and grace, wholeness and holiness.

FOR REFLECTION

- Does doubt have any place in an authentic relationship with God? Why or why not? Do you believe that God can help a person find a faith of their own? If so, how?
- The chapter mentions a few misperceptions people often have about who God is. Do you identify with any of these? If so, how? If not, what misperceptions of God's character have you experienced?

- If someone were to ask you why a person needs God, what would you say and why?
- In specific terms, how do you see God as the only one who can truly fulfill our compulsion for completion? If you don't agree with this position, why not?
- What does it mean to you when this chapter says the only way to relate to God without feeling phony is to do so with integrity? What does integrity mean to you?

Notes

INTRODUCTION: Our Longing for Belonging

1. David G. Myers, *The Pursuit of Happiness* (New York: Avon Books, 1992).

2. Tori DeAngelis, "A Nation of Hermits: The Loss of Community," *The American Psychological Association Monitor* (September 1995): 45–46.

3. Chip Walker and Elissa Moses, "The Age of Self-Navigation," *American Demographics* (September 1996): 38.

4. Bridget Murray, "College Youth Haunted by Increased Pressures," *The American Psychological Association Monitor* (April 1996): 47.

5. Ashley Montegue, "A Scientist Looks at Love," *Phi Delta Kappa* 11, no. 9 (May 1970): 463–67.

6. David W. Smith, *Men Without Friends* (Nashville: Nelson, 1990), 46–47.

7. Jerry Seinfeld, *SeinLanguage* (New York: Bantam, 1995).

CHAPTER ONE: The Compulsion for Completion

1. George Herbert Mead, *Mind, Self, and Society* (Chicago: University of Chicago Press, 1934), 164.

2. Ingri D'Aulaire and Edgar Parin D'Aulaire, *D'Aulaire's Book of Greek Myths* (New York: Doubleday & Co., 1962), 74–75.

3. Dov P. Elkins, *Glad to Be Me* (New York: Prentice-Hall, 1976), 28–29.

4. Aaron Stern, M.D., *Me: The Narcissistic American* (New York: Ballantine, 1979), 28. The study is also summarized in Daniel Goldman's *Emotional Intelligence* (New York: Bantam, 1995).

5. Uichi Shoda, Walter Mischel, and Philip K. Peake, "Predicting Adolescent Cognitive and Self-regulatory Competencies From Preschool Delay of Gratification," *Developmental Psychology*, 26, 6 (1990): 978–86.

6. M. Scott Peck, *The Road Less Traveled* (New York: Simon and Schuster, 1978), 19.

7. Larry Crabb, *The Marriage Builder* (Grand Rapids: Zondervan, 1992).

8. Psalm 73:26

9. 1 John 4:12

CHAPTER TWO: Keeping Family Ties from Pulling Strings

1. Theodor Lidz, *The Person* (New York: Basic Books, 1983).

2. T. Berry Brazelton, *Heart Start: The Emotional Foundations of School Readiness* (Arlington, Va.: National Center for Clinical Infant Programs, 1992).

3. R. W. Bradley, "Using Sibling Dyads to Understand Career Development," *The Personnel and Guidance Journal* 62 (1984): 397–400.

4. Albert Bandura, *Social Foundations of Thought and Action: A Social-Cognitive Theory* (Englewood Cliffs, N.J.: Prentice-Hall, 1986).

CHAPTER THREE: Crossing the Gender Line

1. E. Maccoby and C. N. Jacklin, "Gender Segregation in Childhood," in H. Reese, ed., *Advances in Child Development and Behavior* (New York: Academic Press, 1987).

2. J. Gottman, "Same and Cross-sex Friendship in Young Children," in J. Gottman and J. Parker, eds., *Conversation of Friends* (New York: Cambridge University Press, 1986).

3. Robert Bly, quoted in Gloria Bird and Michael Sporakowski, *Taking Sides: Clashing Views on Controversial Issues in Family and Personal Relationships* (3rd ed.) (Guilford, Conn.: William C. Brown Publishers, 1996).

4. L. R. Brody and J. A. Hall, "Gender and Emotion," in Michael Lews and Jeannette Haviland, eds., *Handbook of Emotions* (New York: Guilford Press, 1993).

5. Deborah Tannen, *You Just Don't Understand* (New York: Ballantine, 1991).

6. Carol Gilligan, *In a Different Voice: Psychological Theory and Women's Development* (Cambridge, Mass.: Harvard University Press, 1982).

7. Ibid.

8. L. A. Sapadin, "Friendship and Gender: Perspectives of Professional Men and Women," *Journal of Social and Personal Relationships* 5 (1988): 387–403.

9. W. K. Rawlins, "Cross-sex Friendship and Communicative Management of Sex-role Expectations," *Communication Quarterly* 30 (1982): 343–52.

CHAPTER FOUR: Friends to Die For

1. "Friends Survey," *Self Magazine* (June 1995): 108.

2. Genesis 2:18 NKJV.

3. Tori DeAngelis, "A Nation of Hermits: The Loss of Community," *The American Psychological Association Monitor* (September 1995): 45–46.

4. S. W. Duck, *Understanding Relationships* (New York: Guildford, 1991).

5. Aristotle, *The Ethics of Aristotle: The Nichomachean Ethics*, rev. ed., trans. J. A. K. Thomson (Harmondsworth, England: Penguin Books, 1976).

6. 1 Samuel 18:3.

7. K. E. Davis and M. J. Todd, "Assessing Friendship: Prototypes, Paradigm Cases, and Relationship Description," in S. W. Duck and D. Perlman, eds., *Understanding Personal Relationships* (London: Sage, 1985), 17–38.

8. C. R. Rogers, G.T. Gendlin, D. V. Kiesler, and C. B. Traus, *The Therapeutic Relationship and Its Impact* (Madison, Wis.: University of Wisconsin Press, 1967).

9. F. Dickson-Harkman, "Self-disclosure with Friends Across the Lifecycle," *Journal of Social and Personal Relationships* 3 (1986): 259–64.

10. C. S. Lewis, *The Four Loves* (New York: Harcourt Brace Jovanovich, 1960).

11. Cicero, Marcus Tullius, *De Amicitia* (New York: Century Company, 1898).

CHAPTER FIVE: What to Do When Friends Fail

1. W. W. Hartup, "Conflict and Friendship Relations," in C. U. Shantz and W. W. Hartup, eds., *Conflict in Child and Adolescent Development* (Cambridge, England: Cambridge University Press, 1993), 186–215.

2. S. W. Duck and J. T. Wood, "For Better, for Worse, for Richer, for Poorer: The Rough and the Smooth of Relationships," in S. W. Duck and J. T. Wood, eds., *Confronting Relationship Challenges* (Thousand Oaks, Calif.: Sage, 1995): 1–21.

3. Romans 12:17.

CHAPTER SIX: Falling in Love Without Losing Your Mind

1. Marilyn French, *The Women's Room* (New York: HarperCollins, 1977), 10.

2. M. Attridge, E. Berscheid, and J. A. Simpson, "Predicting Relationship Stability from Both Partners Versus One," *Journal of Personality and Social Psychology* 69 (1995): 254–68.

3. J. Quittner, "Boy Meets Badge," *Time* (October 28, 1996): 87.

4. E. Walster, V. Aronson, D. Abrahams, and L. Rottmann, "Importance of Physical Attractiveness in Dating Behavior," *Journal of Personality and Social Psychology* 4 (1966): 508–16.

5. J. A. Simpson and S. W. Gangestad, "Socio-sexuality and Romantic Partner Choice," *Journal of Personality* 60 (1992): 31–51.

6. R. J. Sternberg, *The Triangle of Love: Intimacy, Passion, Commitment* (New York: Basic Books, 1988).

7. Amos 3:3 KJV.

8. Z. Rubin, L. A. Peplau, and C. Hill, "Loving and Leaving: Sex Differences in Romantic Attachments," *Sex Roles* 7 (1981): 821–35.

9. J. K. Antill, "Sex Role Complementarity Versus Similarity in Married Couples," *Journal of Personality and Social Psychology* 45 (1983): 145–55.

10. J. Baudrillard, *Cool Memories* (New York: HarperCollins, 1990), 3.

CHAPTER SEVEN: Sex, Lies, and the Great Escape

1. "Sins of the Fathers," *U.S. News and World Report* (August 14, 1995): 51–52.

2. Quoted in "Sex with a Scorecard" by Jill Smolowe, *Time* (April 5, 1993): 41.

3. J. P. Shapiro, "Teenage Sex: Just Say 'Wait,'" *U.S. News and World Report* (July 26, 1993): 56.

4. Have you ever wondered why the most sexually desirable and liberated people on earth—celebrities—seem to have the most difficulty with lasting relationships? Think about it. When we learn of a Hollywood wedding between two stars, most of us wonder how long it will last. Why? Because you can't build a relationship on physical attractiveness and sex.

5. Lewis Smedes, *Sex for Christians* (Grand Rapids: Eerdmans, 1976): 130.

6. The survey was commissioned by the Family Research Council and data was collected from a nationwide random telephone sample of 1,100 people and conducted by an independent Bethesda firm and analyzed by an American University psychologist. Reported by William R Mattox, Jr., in "The Hottest Valentines," *The Washington Post* (1994).

7. R. T. Michael, J. H. Gagnon, and E. O. Lauman, *Sex in America: A Definitive Survey* (Boston: Little, Brown & Co., 1994), 124.

8. Michael et al, 125.

9. L. H. Bukstel, G. D. Roeder, P. R. Kilmann, J. Laughlin, and W. Sotile, "Projected Extramarital Sexual Involvement in Unmarried College Students," *Journal of Marriage and the Family* 40 (1978): 337–40.

10. Quoted by William R. Mattox, Jr., in "The Hottest Valentines," *The Washington Post* (1994).

11. J. E. Stets, "The Link Between Past and Present Intimate Relationships," *Journal of Family Issues* 114 (1993): 251.

12. M. D. Newcomb and P. M. Bentler, "Assessment of Personality and Demographic Aspects of Cohabitation and Marital Success," *Journal of Personality Assessment* 44 (1980): 21.

13. W. Axinn and A. Thorton, "The Relationship Between Cohabitation and Divorce: Selectivity or Casual Influence?" *Demography* 29 (1992): 358.

14. R. M. Cate, E. Long, J. J. Angera, and K. K. Draper, "Sexual Intercourse and Relationship Development," *Family Relations* 42 (1993): 158–64.

15. See 1 Corinthians 7:1–2; 1 Thessalonians 4:3–7; Hebrews 13:4; Matthew 15:18–20; Ephesians 5:3; and 1 Corinthians 6:9.

16. Quoted in "Why I'm a Virgin," by Mark Moring, *Campus Life* (May/June, 1994): 19.

17. Today three quarters of boys and half of girls have had sex by the time they graduate high school. "Virgin Cool," *Newsweek* (October 17, 1994): 61.

18. Isaiah 1:18.

CHAPTER EIGHT: Breaking Up Without Falling Apart

1. L. Baxter, "Gender Differences in the Heterosexual Relationship Rules Embedded in Breakup Accounts," *Journal of Social and Personal Relationships* 3 (1986): 289–306.

2. R. F. Baumeister, S. R. Wotman, and A. M. Stillwell, "Unrequited Love: On Heartbreak, Anger, Guilt, Scriptlessness, and Humiliation," *Journal of Personality and Social Psychology* 64 (1993): 377–87.

3. Baumeister, et al, 377–87.

4. P. Shaver, C. Hazan, and D. Bradshaw, "Love as Attachment: The Integration of Three Behavioral Systems," in R. J. Sternberg and M. L. Barnes, eds., *The Psychology of Love* (New Haven, Conn.: Yale University Press, 1988), 68–99.

5. P. Kramer, "Should You Leave?" *Psychology Today* (September 1997): 38–45.

6. W. Berman, "The Role of Attachment in the Post-Divorce Experience," *Journal of Personality and Social Psychology* 54 (1988): 496–503.

7. C. Riessman, *Divorce Talk: Women and Men Make Sense of Personal Relationships* (New Brunswick, N.J.: Rutgers University Press, 1980).

8. C. T. Hill, Z. Rubin, and L. A. Peplau, "Breakups Before Marriage: The End of 103 Affairs," *Journal of Social Issues* 32 (1976): 147–68.

9. S. S. Brehm, *Intimate Relationships*, 2nd ed. (New York: McGraw-Hill, 1992).

10. G. B. Spanier and L. Thompson, *Parting: The Aftermath of Separation and Divorce* (Beverly Hills, Calif.: Sage, 1984). Research has shown that men tend to fall in love more quickly than women, and women tend to fall out of love more readily than men. Experts suggest two explanations for women initiating breakups more often. First, women are more discriminating in dating than men, and second, women are more sensitive than men to the quality of interpersonal relationships. Hence, their standards for developing love may be higher than men's. A woman may experience lack of rapport or self-revelation in a relationship, for example, while the man does not. As a result, women may evaluate and reevaluate their relationships more carefully.

11. A. Holtzqorth-Munroe and N. S. Jacobson, "Causal Attributions of Married Couples: When Do They Search for Causes? What Do They Conclude When They Do?" *Journal of Personality and Social Psychology* 48 (1985): 1398–1412.

12. E. Kübler-Ross, *On Death and Dying* (New York: Macmillan, 1969); and E. Kübler-Ross, "The Dying Patient's Point of View," in O. G. Brim Jr., H. E. Freeman, S. Levine, and N. A. Scotch, eds., *The Dying Patient* (New York: Russell Sage Foundation, 1970).

13. J. Bowlby, *Attachment and Loss*, Volume 3, *Loss* (New York: Basic Books, 1980).

CHAPTER NINE: Relating to God Without Feeling Phony

1. E. Wiesel, *Night* (New York: Bantam, 1960), 71–72.

2. S. Freud, *Totem and Taboo* (New York: Norton, 1950). See also Sigmund Freud, *The Future of an Illusion* (New York: Norton, 1961).

3. E. Durkheim, *The Elementary Forms of the Religious Life*, trans. Joseph Ward Swain (New York: Free Press, 1965).

4. See Romans 1:21–25.

5. John 3:16.

6. 1 John 4:16.

7. 1 John 4:19.

8. Mark 1:1; Matthew 3:17; Luke 3:22.

relationships
workbook

Contents

How to Use This Workbook

Too often, reading a book can lead to great ideas, but little action. This workbook is meant to change all that. Its self-tests and exercises will help you put feet on the ideas you have while reading *Relationships*. And we believe you'll enjoy it. As Shakespeare said, "Joy's soul lies in the doing."

While this workbook will become a rather personal record of your own exploration—and while it is designed to be used on your own—we have also written it to be used in group settings. In other words, you may want to do the self-tests and exercises while reading each chapter on your own, and then take time to discuss the questions with others after completing the chapter (this makes for a convenient nine- or ten-week classroom or small-group series). Interacting with others on this material will not only help you compare and contrast your varying viewpoints, it will help you better define and articulate your own perspective.

Each chapter contains four specific self-tests or exercises to tap into a particular idea you are reading about. We suggest pausing as you make your way through each chapter and doing the recommended exercises at that particular time. Following the four chapter exercises are a half-dozen discussion questions for small groups. Each section concludes with suggestions for further study of the chapter's topic by recommending other relationship resources.

As you work through the pages of this book, make it your own. Don't get too hung up on following the rules. If a particular exercise leads your down a more intriguing path, take it. Some of these exercises may simply serve as springboards to discussions that more appropriately fit your style. However, if an exercise seems a bit challenging, don't give up on it. As the saying goes, anything worth having is worth working for. In any case, we pray you will enjoy your journey toward making bad relationships better and good relationships great.

Les and Leslie Parrott
Center for Relationship Development
Seattle Pacific University

exercises

for

chapter one

The Compulsion
for Completion

Your Relational Readiness

The following self-test will take about five minutes and will help you assess your relational "readiness." Answer each item by using the following scale to indicate the degree to which it is true for you:

4 — Often
3 — Sometimes
2 — Rarely
1 — Never

____ I feel a sense of relief when I don't have to be alone.

____ Any relationship is better than nothing.

____ If I'm not in a dating relationship, I feel less desirable.

____ I experience a little bit of panic when I think of not having someone to be close to.

____ The very idea of solitude strikes fear in my heart.

____ I'm tempted to settle for most any relationship because I don't know if I can find anyone better.

____ My romantic relationships are more of an issue of being selected rather than doing the selecting.

____ When I am dating someone else I feel better about myself.

____ I don't like to be alone.

____ I don't have a very clear idea of the personal qualities I look for in a person to date or even to be friends with.

____ Total Score

Scoring: Add the numbers you have placed beside each item. There is a possible total of forty points. To interpret your score, use the following scale:

40–30 A score in this range is a strong indicator of your need to establish a healthier sense of your identity and personal wholeness. You will want to pay special attention to the four steps toward wholeness discussed in this chapter.

29–20 A score in this range indicates that you have done some significant work in establishing a healthy identity and a good sense of self-worth.

You still have more work to do, however, in constructing an integrated and whole sense of self that will help to ensure healthier relationships.

19–1   A score in this range indicates an established sense of security in who you are and a confident perspective on your sense of personal wholeness. This should serve you well in your relationships.

Healing Your Primal Pain

This exercise can take as little as fifteen minutes to much longer and will require a place for quiet contemplation and self-exploration. You may want to use additional paper for this exercise.

- Reflect on your personal history and make note of any memories you have of feeling abandoned or neglected (even if they seem fairly insignificant).

_____

_____

_____

_____

- Are there people from your past or present that you blame for not being there for you? Who are they and what do you blame them for?

_____

_____

_____

- As you review these painful moments from your past, do you see ways in which they may still be impacting your present? In what ways are they determining choices you are making when it comes to your relationships?

_____

_____

_____

_____

- Are you able to forgive whoever is involved in your painful memories? Are you able to release any resentment you may be holding onto? What might you need to do to take care of your "unfinished business"?

_____

_____

_____

_____

If you are carrying a great deal of personal pain from your past and not finding resolution for it in the present, you could probably benefit greatly from seeking the help of a trusted friend, minister, or counselor.

Taking Off Your Masks

This exercise will take about ten minutes and will help you become more aware of the masks you sometimes use to guard against feeling judged or negatively evaluated. It focuses on three areas: work, home, and church; if you'd like to add another, feel free.

I wear masks at work (or school):

Very Often   *Almost Never*

1   2   3   4   5   6   7

If your answer was between one and four, describe the kinds of masks you wear at work (or school) and with whom.

_____

_____

_____

I wear masks at home:

Very Often   *Almost Never*

1   2   3   4   5   6   7

If your answer was between one and four, describe the kinds of masks you wear at home and with whom.

_____

_____

_____

I wear masks at church:

Very Often   *Almost Never*

1   2   3   4   5   6   7

If your answer was between one and four, describe the kinds of masks you wear at church and with whom.

_____

_____

_____

Now review your responses and determine which of your masks serves
a helpful function and which ones you think may be interfering with your ability to cultivate healthy relationships. What can you do to discard these
unhealthy masks?

_____

_____

exercise four

Designing Your Destiny

    This exercise will take about fifteen minutes or more. It is designed to help you construct a personal statement of purpose and create goals that will help you fulfill it.

    To begin with, take a moment to determine what you value. It will be difficult, but force yourself to rank the following twelve values (1 = most important to you).

_____ Achievement: Feeling satisfaction for a job well done.

_____ Challenges: Using your creativity, training, and intelligence to face challenges.

_____ Education: Increasing your intellectual understanding of life.

_____ Aesthetic Considerations: Appreciating the beauty in people, art, or nature.

_____ Health: Feeling good in a physical and emotional sense.

_____ Independence: Having freedom to do your own thing.

_____ Morality: Maintaining your moral, ethical, and religious standards.

_____ Pleasure: Having time to play and have a good time.

_____ Relationships: Caring for, sharing with, and giving to those who are close to you.

_____ Spirituality: Cultivating a meaningful and personal relationship with God.

_____ Security: Feeling safe, free from unexpected and unpleasant changes.

_____ Service to Others: Knowing you have benefited others.

_____ Wealth: Improving your financial position.

    As you ponder what matters most to you, consider how your top three or four values can be incorporated into a personal purpose statement. This statement does not need to be permanent (it will change throughout your life). Just draft something that seems right for you at this time—something that is personally compelling and comes from the heart.

My purpose is . . . _____

_____

Once you've drafted your purpose statement, note some specific and obtainable goals that can serve as a means to fulfill it.

Short-term goals (obtainable within the next three or four months):

1. _____

2. _____

3. _____

Long-term goals (obtainable within the next year or more):

1. _____

2. _____

3. _____

In what specific ways will you need to delay your immediate gratification in order to enjoy the benefits of meeting your goals?

_____

_____

_____

The Compulsion for Completion

The following questions are to help facilitate a meaningful small-group discussion. Feel free to explore different territory, but don't veer too far off track. In the space provided, jot down some of the group's responses to these questions. And remember, anyone is always free to "pass" on any particular question without explanation.

1. Describe your experience of completing the exercises for this chapter. What did you learn about yourself?

   _____

   _____

   _____

   _____

2. What do you make of the idea that it is only when we no longer compulsively need someone that we can ever attempt to build a healthy relationship with them? Do you agree? Why or why not?

   _____

   _____

   _____

   _____

3. Of the two lies discussed in this chapter which do you encounter more often: (1) I need this person to be complete; or (2) If this person needs me, I'll be complete?

   _____

   _____

   _____

   _____

4. How willing and comfortable are you to disclose yourself to others and let yourself be known by others? What social masks do you sometimes wear that guard you against being vulnerable? When are you most likely to wear them?

_____

_____

_____

_____

5. On a scale of one to ten, how would you rate your current tendency to delay immediate gratification? If you do this well, what's your secret? If you're striving to do this better, how can you improve?

_____

_____

_____

_____

6. It's easy to rely on another person instead of God to meet your deepest needs. Why do you think most of us struggle with this idea?

_____

_____

_____

_____

The Compulsion for Completion

To explore more of what the Bible has to say about this topic, consider the following passages:

- 1 John 4:7–21 talks about how our love for one another is predicated on God's love of us.

_____

_____

_____

- Colossians 1:19–22 talks about how God accepts us like no human can.

_____

_____

_____

- Ephesians 4:14 and 2 Corinthians 10:7 talk about our feeble attempts to find significance in surface things.

_____

_____

_____

Other books that may be of interest to you on this topic include:

- *The Search for Significance* by Robert S. McGee (Houston: Rapha, 1990).
    This book explores how we can build our self-worth on our ability to please others—or on the love and forgiveness of God. It will help you explore your goals, your motives, and your sense of identity. You will learn how to get off the performance treadmill and discover why personal success, status, beauty, and wealth do not bring lasting happiness.

- *The Road Less Traveled* by M. Scott Peck (New York: Simon and Schuster, 1977).

   On the *New York Times* best-seller's list for years, this book has become a classic for exploring personal growth issues such as delayed gratification, responsibility, emotional management, and other disciplines. Confronting and solving personal problems is a painful process that most of us try to avoid. This book may help you move beyond avoidance to actually make some changes.

- *The Marriage Builder* by Larry Crabb (Grand Rapids: Zondervan, 1992).

   Although this book is specifically for married couples, it has plenty of relevance for anyone wanting to learn more about how our deepest needs cannot be satisfied by another person, only through God (especially chapter 2).

exercises

for

chapter two

Keeping
Family Ties
from
Pulling Strings

exercise five

How Healthy Is Your Home?

This exercise will take about ten minutes and will help you assess the health of your home. Understand that no family is perfect. But some families are healthier than others. In fact, Dolores Curran, in her book *Traits of a Healthy Family* (Ballantine, 1983), unveils the results of a study identifying the top fifteen traits noted again and again by family experts. They are noted below.

Using the following scale, rate the degree to which your family is characterized by these desirable traits.

4 — Much of the time
3 — Some of the time
2 — Rarely
1 — Almost never

_____ Communicates and listens
_____ Affirms and supports one another
_____ Teaches respect for others
_____ Develops a sense of trust
_____ Has a sense of play and humor
_____ Exhibits a sense of shared responsibility
_____ Teaches a sense of right and wrong
_____ Has a strong sense of family in which rituals and traditions abound
_____ Has a balance of interaction among members
_____ Has a shared religious core
_____ Respects the privacy of one another
_____ Values service to others
_____ Fosters family table time and conversation
_____ Shares leisure time
_____ Admits to and seeks help with problems
_____ Total

Scoring: Add the numbers you have placed beside each item. There is a possible total of sixty points. To interpret your score, use the following:

50–60   Count your blessings. You grew up in a relatively loving home free of dysfunction. Mom and Dad took time to nurture your development and cultivate an atmosphere that was positive and caring. Your relationships will certainly benefit from this good foundation.

30–49   Your family health falls into the midrange, or average zone. Your family may not be all you'd like it to be, but then again, things could be a lot worse. You will want to learn from the tensions and disengaged style that is sometimes present in your home. How do you contribute to it, and what can you do to make the relationships better?

1–29   This range, unfortunately, is where you will find families with the most strife. Perhaps you have experienced a lot of distressed and polarized relationships (even abusive ones) at home. If so, this will present some challenges to your present and future relationships, but nothing that can't be overcome with good relational skills.

Uncovering Unspoken Rules

This exercise will take about ten or fifteen minutes and will help you pinpoint the unspoken rules you absorbed from your family of origin.

Take your time to complete the following sentence stems. Simply complete them by writing the first thing that pops into your head:

• Men should . . . _____

_____

• Women should . . . _____

_____

• Success is . . . _____

_____

• The most important thing . . . _____

_____

• Life . . . _____

_____

Now review what you have written and edit it to conform to how you believe your parents would have completed these sentences. This will give you a pretty good start at uncovering your family's unspoken rules. Use the space below to write down any additional rules that may not have been articulated, but were still known.

_____

_____

_____

_____

In what specific ways will your family's unspoken rules influence your relationships?

_____

Lessons Learned from Mom and Dad

We all learn by example, especially when that example is Mom and Dad. In the following relationship skill areas, note how each of your parents (or primary caretakers) behaved. You might rate their effectiveness on a scale of one to ten and then write a brief description of how each performed in that skill. This exercise will take about ten to fifteen minutes.

	Your Mother	Your Father
Talking about their experiences		
Showing their feelings		
Standing up for themselves		
Being a good listener		
Understanding other's perspectives		
Managing anger		
Accepting responsibility (not passing the buck)		
Working for equitable solutions		

exercise eight

If Your Parents Got Divorced

This exercise will take about ten minutes and will help you apply the principles discussed in the chapter.

Take a moment to list the things you have done to come to terms with your parents' divorce. In specific terms, what have you done to bring personal healing to the pain it has caused you? What things have helped the most?

_____

_____

_____

_____

How well are you managing your anger?

Not so well   *Very Well*

   1   2   3   4   5   6   7

If this is not going so well, what specific steps can you take to get it under control?

_____

_____

How well are you managing conflict-avoidance?

Not so well   *Very Well*

   1   2   3   4   5   6   7

If this is not going so well, what specific steps can you take to express your genuine feelings—even when they may cause conflict?

_____

_____

How would you rate the strength of your self-confidence?

Not so strong   *Very strong*

   1   2   3   4   5   6   7

If your self-confidence is not too strong, what specific steps can you take to build it up?

_____

_____

As you review this exercise, consider your overall health in the aftermath of your parents' divorce. If it is not getting better for you, we urge you to seek help from a competent counselor, a compassionate minister, or even a concerned friend. The strength of all your other relationships depends on it.

Keeping Family Ties
from Pulling Strings

The following questions are to help facilitate a meaningful small-group discussion. Feel free to explore different territory, but don't veer too far off track. In the space provided, jot down some of the group's responses to these questions. And remember, anyone is always free to "pass" on any particular question without explanation.

1. Describe your experience of completing the exercises for this chapter. What did you learn about yourself?

   _____

   _____

   _____

   _____

2. Can you think of another social force that has had more power in shaping your life than the family? Why or why not?

   _____

   _____

   _____

   _____

3. In what specific ways has your family of origin shaped your personality, your career choice, your relationships, your values?

   _____

   _____

   _____

   _____

4. In what specific ways does your family still "pull your strings"? In other words, how do your early family influences still manifest themselves in your present relationships?

_____

_____

_____

_____

5. Of the three major ways families shape us—rules, roles, and relationships—which one do you see as the most influential and why? Can you think of an example to underscore your reasoning?

_____

_____

_____

_____

6. If your parents are divorced, how do you think that may impact future relationships? Think of both challenges and advantages.

_____

_____

_____

_____

for further study
of chapter two

Keeping Family Ties
from Pulling Strings

To explore more of what the Bible has to say about this topic, consider the following passages:

• 1 Kings 22 is just one biblical example of how powerful the family's impact is.

_____

_____

_____

• Ephesians 5:21–33 talks about the relationship of husbands and wives, the architects of every family.

_____

_____

_____

• Romans 8:28 gives encouraging words for everyone who has not had the greatest home life.

_____

_____

_____

Other books that may be of interest to you on this topic include:

• *Intimate Worlds: Life Inside the Family* by Maggie Scarf (New York: Random House, 1995).
    This is a serious examination of the complexities of families. The author combines clear analysis with meaningful stories to expose the core issues that every family must deal with.

- *The Tribute* by Dennis Rainey and David Boehi (Nashville: Thomas Nelson, 1994).

    If you are looking for ways to develop a more meaningful relationship with your parents, this book can serve as your guide to resolving issues from the past and blessing your parents in the present.

- *Family Shock* by Gary R. Collins (Wheaton: Tyndale, 1995).

    This book is filled with expert analysis, true stories, and practical advice on keeping families strong in the midst of earthshaking change. This one doesn't shy away from tough topics, and it imparts an uplifting and optimistic message about families.

exercises
for
chapter three

Crossing
the
Gender Line

What's Your Gender I.Q.?

This exercise will take about five minutes and will help you get a general idea of how much you already know about some fundamental differences between the genders. Answer each of the following items as either true or false.

1. T F Women are better spellers than men.

2. T F Men are more likely than women to use conversation to solve problems.

3. T F Women have larger connections between their brain's left and right hemispheres.

4. T F Men are better at reading the emotions of others than women are.

5. T F Men score higher on the math section of the SAT than do women.

6. T F In comparison to men, women are better at maintaining a sense of geographical direction.

7. T F Men are better than women at fitting suitcases into a crowded car trunk.

8. T F Women are better than men at describing their feelings.

9. T F Men, more than women, focus their energy on achievement.

10. T F Women, more than men, give priority to relationships.

Scoring: Each of these items is based on current gender research studies. Note how many of the items you got correct. 1-T, 2-T, 3-T, 4-F, 5-T, 6-F, 7-T, 8-T, 9-T, 10-T. The higher your score, the better your base knowledge of gender differences.

What If You Were the Opposite Sex?

This exercise can take as little as fifteen minutes to much longer. As strange and as difficult as this might seem, do your best to imagine what it would be like to live as the opposite sex. In other words, if you are a man, what would life be like for you if you were a woman? And if you are a woman, what would it be like to live as a man? With this in mind, answer the following questions as honestly as you can.

1. What is your first reaction to living as the opposite sex?

   _____

   _____

   _____

2. How would the simple task of getting ready in the morning be different if you were the opposite gender (e.g., the time it would take, what you would do, how you would dress)?

   _____

   _____

   _____

3. How would living as the opposite sex affect your career choice and other aspirations?

   _____

   _____

   _____

4. As the opposite gender, would you feel more or less safe in society? Why?

   _____

   _____

   _____

5. Would you feel any different about dating and the prospect of marriage if you were the opposite gender? If so, how?

_____

_____

_____

6. How would your relationship with both your mom and dad differ if you were the opposite gender?

_____

_____

_____

Once you have taken the time to answer these questions, you may find it insightful to share your answers with another person who has completed the same exercise.

A Self-Test for Women Only

This exercise will take about ten minutes and will help you review and apply some important insights in understanding the men in your life. Take a moment to reflect on what the book has to say about "what women need to know about men." For each of the statements below, note an example from your own life that illustrates the point.

Men are not as in touch with their emotions as we are.

_____

_____

_____

Men are more independent than we are.

_____

_____

_____

Men are more abstract than we are.

_____

_____

_____

Next, consider what you can do in practical terms to bridge the gender gap with the most important men in your life. In other words, how can you apply the above insights to these relationships?

_____

_____

_____

_____

_____

exercise twelve

A Self-Test for Men Only

This exercise will take about ten minutes and will help you review and apply some important insights in understanding the women in your life. Take a moment to reflect on what the book has to say about "what men need to know about women." For each of the statements below, note an example from your own life that illustrates the point.

Women are not as independent as we are.

_____

_____

_____

Women focus on the here-and-now more than we do.

_____

_____

_____

Women are not as competitive as we are.

_____

_____

_____

Next, consider what you can do in practical terms to bridge the gender gap with the most important women in your life. In other words, how can you apply the above insights to these relationships?

_____

_____

_____

_____

_____

_____

Crossing the Gender Line

The following questions are to help facilitate a meaningful small-group discussion. Feel free to explore different territory, but don't veer too far off track. In the space provided, jot down some of the group's responses to these questions. And remember, anyone is always free to "pass" on any particular question without explanation.

1. Describe your experience of completing the exercises for this chapter. What did you learn about yourself?

   _____

   _____

   _____

   _____

2. Consider your cross-gender relationships. What aspects of these relationships with the opposite sex (excluding romantic relationships) seem to be easier than relationships with the same sex? What are the biggest hurdles you encounter in relating with the opposite sex?

   _____

   _____

   _____

   _____

3. When you were growing up as a kid, what social activities or games do you think influenced your gender roles? Looking back on it, do you put more stock in the way your environment shaped you or the way your biology programmed you?

   _____

   _____

   _____

   _____

4. This chapter notes several things men and women should know about the opposite gender. What differences could you add?

_____

_____

_____

_____

5. Have you noticed how women use their conversation to build "rapport" while men use conversation to give or get the "report"? What examples of this disparity can you remember from your own experience?

_____

_____

_____

_____

6. The major point of this chapter is that we doom our relationships with the opposite sex when we try to change them into being more like us. If this is so, what can you do to accept and even appreciate the different qualities of the other gender?

_____

_____

_____

_____

Crossing the Gender Line

To explore more of what the Bible has to say about this topic, consider the following passages:

- Genesis 1:27 talks of both male and female being created in the image of God.

_____

_____

_____

- Galatians 3:28 instructs us in the equality and unity of the genders before God in Christ.

_____

_____

_____

- Ephesians 4:4–8 reminds us that although we each have been given different gifts, we are one in Christ.

_____

_____

_____

Other books that may be of interest to you on this topic include:

- *Men & Women: Enjoying the Difference* by Larry Crabb (Grand Rapids: Zondervan, 1991).

    According to psychologist Larry Crabb, men and women share a deadly problem that kills good relating. The problem is this: we are committed, first of all, to ourselves. Each of us, without blushing, holds fast to an overriding concern for our own well-being. Giving numerous examples from his counseling office, Crabb explores how we can turn away from ourselves and toward each other, how we can become what he calls "other-centered."

- *Men Are from Mars, Women Are from Venus* by John Gray (New York: HarperCollins, 1992).

  Using his now famous metaphor to illustrate the commonly occurring conflicts between men and women, John Gray explains how gender differences can come between the sexes and prohibit mutually fulfilling loving relationships. He gives advice on how to counteract these differences in communication styles, emotional needs, and modes of behavior to promote a greater understanding between individuals.

- *Can Men and Women Be Just Friends?* by Andy Bustanoby (Grand Rapids: Zondervan, 1993).

  This helpful book helps both men and women understand what friendship is and how to handle opposite-sex friendships. Bustanoby explains that friendships between the opposite sex are possible with certain boundaries, and he carefully outlines these boundaries in the book.

exercises
for
chapter four

Friends
to Die For

The Friendship Assessment

This exercise will help you evaluate the current condition of each of your friendships. It will take about ten minutes or so, depending on how many friendships you evaluate.

Have a specific friend in mind and then answer each of the following true and false questions as honestly as you can.

T F   This person knows how to keep a secret.

T F   We can disagree and then make up without holding grudges.

T F   This person almost always makes time for me, and I do the same for him/her.

T F   When he/she gives me advice, it is generally without judgment.

T F   I can totally be myself around this person.

T F   He/she is a good listener.

T F   This person has stuck by me through tough times and is willing to make personal sacrifices for me.

T F   This person knows my faults, but loves me anyway.

T F   Our relationship is balanced with give and take; we are equally vulnerable and caring.

T F   I am able to set clear boundaries with this person when necessary and he/she respects them.

T F   No subject is off-limits in our conversation.

T F   I can always count on this person.

_____ Total number of "T" responses for . . .

_____ Total number of "T" responses for . . .

_____ Total number of "T" responses for . . .

_____ Total number of "T" responses for . . .

Scoring: Add up the number of true responses you have for each friendship you evaluated. There is a possible total of twelve points for each relationship. To interpret your score, use the following:

10–12   No doubt about it, this is a good friend who is worth all the effort, care, and investment. You will want to do all that you can to nurture this relationship and enjoy it.

7–9   Although this person could be more sensitive to your needs, this amigo shows great potential. Be careful, however, not to set yourself up for disappointment if this person doesn't meet all your expectations.

0–6   This friend is probably too fair-weather to see you through stormy times (and maybe even the sunny ones, too). Don't hang all your hopes on this one.

exercise fourteen

Are You a "Growth Promoting" Listener?

Most of us have a lot of room for improvement when it comes to learning to listen. This exercise will help you assess your strengths and areas for growth when it comes to this important friendship skill. It will take about five or ten minutes.

It is important that you be honest in answering each of the following three items. Each one asks you about one of the primary aspects of what Carl Rogers called "growth promoting" listening. Simply circle the number that most accurately indicates where you would be on the continuums.

Generally speaking, in meeting someone for the first time at a party, are you *genuinely* interested in getting to know them and understanding their story? Do you really want to know what interests them? Or are you more likely to just go through the motions, being socially appropriate but not very genuine?

Not Genuine   *Extremely Genuine*
   1   2   3   4   5   6   7

Generally speaking, in meeting someone for the first time at a party, are you *accepting* of that person's opinions and feelings? Do you feel open to hearing what they have to say, or are you more likely to interject your opinions and feelings before completely understanding theirs?

Not Accepting   *Extremely Accepting*
   1   2   3   4   5   6   7

Generally speaking, in meeting someone for the first time at a party, are you *empathic* with them? Do you put yourself in their shoes and try to accurately understand their experience, or are you more likely to jump to a few conclusions and make a few assumptions?

Not Empathic   *Extremely Empathic*
   1   2   3   4   5   6   7

_____ Total Score

Scoring and Interpretation: Add up the numbers you have circled. There is a total of twenty-one points possible and the higher your score, the more likely you are to be a "growth promoting" listener. However, you may find it most helpful to consider each continuum separately to see which of the three important qualities you will want to work on most.

Are You a Fair-weather Friend?

This exercise will take about five minutes and will help you assess how loyal you are to your friends. Consider what your friends would say about you when it comes to the following statements. Answer yes or no to each of these items and be as honest as you can.

My friends would say . . .

Y   N   I always keep my promises.

Y   N   I always stick up for them.

Y   N   I give them grace when they let me down.

Y   N   I am just as likely to genuinely celebrate my friends' successes as I am to comfort them in their disappointments.

Y   N   I am there when they need me.

Y   N   I am ready and willing to lend them a hand.

Y   N   I never gossip about them or talk behind their back.

Y   N   I give them the benefit of the doubt.

Y   N   I hear them out even when I disagree.

Y   N   I stand by them through thick and thin.

Scoring: The more items you honestly responded to with a yes, the more likely you are to be loyal to your friends. If you answered yes to nearly all of the items, however, you probably shouldn't take this quality in yourself for granted. Check in with your pals. Ask them to give you a loyalty checkup by inviting them for honest feedback on how you are doing with being loyal. On the other hand, if you did not answer yes to very many of these items, you may want to talk to your friends about how you can better cultivate this quality. Remember, loyalty is what tops the list of what people appreciate most about their friends, so this is one you will want to spend some time on.

Determining Your Dedication Quotient

How dedicated are you to your friends? This exercise will help you answer this question. It will take as little as ten minutes to much longer, depending on whether you discuss your answers with another person who has done the same exercise.

Consider your closest friendships and think about them as you put yourself in the following scenarios. Indicate how you would respond, and feel free to write your own response to better capture what you would say.

Scenario One

You get a call from one of your good friends at 2:00 A.M. He recently called it quits with someone he has been dating for several months, and now he is having second thoughts.

Do you say . . .

    a. "I can't believe you're calling me at 2:00 A.M. I've got to sleep."

    b. "I am so sorry, but I can't even think clearly at this hour. Let's meet over breakfast."

    c. "Tell me how you're doing."

    d. Other: _____

Scenario Two

One of your good friends is moving to a new apartment on Saturday and asks you to help out by lending a hand and also loaning her your car. You have an important project due on Monday and you were planning on using your weekend to do it. You're also not that crazy about using your car as a moving van.

Do you say . . .

    a. "I'd love to help you, but there is just no possible way."

    b. "I can help you for a couple of hours in the morning, but I've got to work on my project in the afternoon."

c. "No problem. Whatever it takes to help a friend."

d. Other: _____

Scenario Three

One of your good friends shows interest in dating someone you had once dated seriously (for about six months). You currently have no attachments to this person, but you have uneasy feelings about the two of them getting together. Your friend asks you how you feel about it.

Do you say . . .

a. "If you go out, I don't see how we can still be friends."

b. "Sure, I don't mind." (And secretly resent it.)

c. "To be honest, I have funny feelings about it, but I'm not sure why."

d. Other: _____

The point of this exercise is to get you thinking about your level of dedication to your friendships. None of the answers is the only "right" one; there is no objective score to be obtained. You may, however, find it helpful to compare your responses with someone else to get some objective feedback. Ask each other why you chose the answers you did and whether you feel good about them. Consider whether you are more dedicated in certain areas (e.g., during times of immediate crisis) than you are in others. And why you are more dedicated to some friends than you are to others. Finally, if you are feeling like your dedication level is lacking, explore concrete ways you can improve it.

Friends to Die For

The following questions are to help facilitate a meaningful small-group discussion. Feel free to explore different territory, but don't veer too far off track. In the space provided, jot down some of the group's responses to these questions. And remember, anyone is always free to "pass" on any particular question without explanation.

1. Describe your experience of completing the exercises for this chapter. What did you learn about yourself?

_____

_____

_____

_____

2. It has been said that many people audition to be our friends but only a few make the cut. What is it about your friends that caused them to get the part? Did it have more to do with circumstances or personal qualities?

_____

_____

_____

_____

3. The medical benefits of having friends is quite remarkable. What benefits of the less scientific kind do you appreciate? What fruits of friendship do you enjoy the most?

_____

_____

_____

_____

4. Do you agree that generally speaking, our good friends come in two forms: as friends of the road and friends of the heart? Think of an example of a meaningful friendship that did not last. What purpose did it serve in your life or what passage did it see you through?

_____

_____

_____

_____

5. Forgiveness can be one of the most challenging struggles for any relationship. Think of a time when you were either on the receiving or the giving end of forgiveness. What makes it so difficult?

_____

_____

_____

_____

6. Of the four qualities that keep friendships going—loyalty, forgiveness, honesty, and dedication—which one is most important to you and why? What other qualities would you add to this list?

_____

_____

_____

_____

for further study
of chapter four

Friends to Die For

To explore more of what the Bible has to say about this topic, consider the following passages:

- Ruth 1:1–18 talks about a woman who went far beyond what was expected for a friend.

_____

_____

_____

- Job 2:1–13 talks about how true friendship offers comfort when the pain is beyond understanding.

_____

_____

_____

- 2 Timothy 1:1–18 talks about the importance of encouragement in strengthening friendship.

_____

_____

_____

Other books that may be of interest to you on this topic include:

- *Just Friends: The Role of Friendship in Our Lives* by Lillian B. Rubin (New York: Harper & Row, 1985).

  Drawing on years of study, Rubin covers the full range of friendships and their interrelations with kinship, marriage, and romance. She exposes the ambiguity, ambivalence, and contradiction with which friendship in our society is hedged.

- *Making Real Friends in a Phony World* by Jim Conway (Grand Rapids: Zondervan, 1989).

     If you're tired of surface relationships and want to achieve new depth in your relationships with family, coworkers, and fellow Christians, this book will show you what it takes to make—and be—a real friend.

- *The Four Loves* by C. S. Lewis (New York: Harcourt Brace Jovanovich, 1960).

     In this classic book, C. S. Lewis provides a candid, wise, and warmly personal look at four basic kinds of human love—affection, friendship, erotic love, and the love of God. Lewis, among other things, explores the possibilities and problems of friendships between men and women. He reveals the virtues and failings of this human longing, and he also explores the questions of sex, possessiveness, jealousy, pride, and false sentimentality.

exercises
for
chapter five

What to Do When Friends Fail

What You Expect from Friends

This exercise will take about five minutes and will help you clarify what you expect from your closest friends. Answer the following true-and-false items as honestly as you can.

T F I expect my friend to know my faults but accept me anyway.

T F I expect my friend to never break special plans with me—even for a date at the last minute.

T F I expect my close friends to always keep their word on both big and small issues.

T F A really good friend should know how I'm feeling most of the time.

T F I expect my friend to say "I'm sorry" when he or she is wrong.

T F My closest friend should confide in me more than anyone else.

T F I expect my friend to always keep a secret.

T F It is difficult for me to forgive a friend who has hurt me in some way.

T F If we are truly friends, we should hardly ever have much conflict.

T F I expect my friends to never talk behind my back or break a confidence—even about small things.

T F My very closest friend should have no other friendships closer than ours.

T F If a good friend breaks a confidence or fails me in some other way, I am unlikely to give him or her a second or third chance.

T F I expect my friend to never hold a grudge against me.

T F I expect my friend to always admit when he or she is wrong.

If you answered true to any of these items, you are more likely to have very high standards about how your friends should treat you. The more times you answered true, the more you expect from your friends and perhaps the more rigid you are with your expectations.

Learning from
Your Own Failed Friendships

This exercise can take as little as ten minutes. It is designed to help you gain insight into how you can avoid repeating patterns of painful relationships. Take your time as you consider a relationship where a person you trusted failed you in some way, and answer the following questions to help you learn from the failure.

• How long did you know this person, and what brought you together?

_____

• Looking back over your relationship, what kinds of things helped you to believe you could trust him or her?

_____

_____

• In specific terms, what did this person do to "fail" you?

_____

_____

• What percentage of the hurt was due to the following:

Percentage

_____ miscommunication
_____ broken confidence
_____ gossip
_____ neglect
_____ betrayal
_____ uncontrollable change (moving)
_____ personality change
_____ moral choices
_____ other _____

- Take a moment for some serious soul searching and try to assess how much you were responsible for the falling out with this friend. Was there anything you did or didn't do that may have contributed to the problem? If so, what was it?

_____

_____

- Did you ever want to get revenge as a result of the hurt you felt from this relationship, and if so, why? Also, what did you do with your vengeful feelings and what was the result?

_____

_____

- Have you come to a place of healing with the hurt you experienced? If so, what helped bring this about?

_____

_____

- In reviewing the basis for your relationship and the reasons for your fallout, what can you surmise about how to avoid a similar situation in future friendships?

_____

_____

Can This Friendship Be Saved?

This exercise will take about five to ten minutes and is designed to help you assess the status of an increasingly troublesome friendship. Consider your particular relationship and take a moment to answer yes or no to the following questions.

Y N You find that one of you is always saying, after the other says hello, "Sorry I didn't get back to you, I've been so busy."

Y N You've made a date with a friend and later schedule another appointment at the same time without realizing it.

Y N You find you talk more about your friend to others than you do to your friend.

Y N When you get together with your friend, you find yourself sitting silently, refusing to ask how she is, and you realize that you're waiting for her to first ask you how you are; it doesn't happen.

Y N You don't like yourself after you've been with him, because he can bring out the worst in you.

Y N You realize that you no longer feel safe being completely honest with her about your personal life.

Y N You're losing patience with his chronic lateness and are frequently mumbling "I've had it" under your breath.

Y N You've reminisced about the past for the fifth straight time and realize that there's an increasing lack of current history between you.

Y N You've talked to your friend about how you feel hurt or neglected and yet there are no signs of positive change.

Y N You feel forced by the relationship to compromise your principles or subvert your self-respect.

_____ Number of yes responses

If you circled yes on three or more of the above statements, your friendship needs work. But unfortunately, it might be beyond repair. Some betrayals are just too big to forgive and forget. Some friendships are so flawed they constantly weigh you down. Other times friends simply outgrow each other. While no one but you can make the decision whether or not to end a friendship, if you've circled yes on most of the above items, you shouldn't ignore the option.

exercise twenty

Making Amends

This exercise can take as much as fifteen minutes or longer. While it may appear to be somewhat rigid or systematic, please do not let it keep you from doing whatever your heart is telling you to do to make amends with the person you care about. Consider these steps as guidelines to help you bring healing and restoration to a floundering friendship.

Step One: Count the Cost

What is the price you are paying to keep this friendship alive? If you were forced to choose between the following two statements, which one would best describe how you feel about this friendship?

1. This friendship has redeeming qualities I value and is worth the cost of repairing and maintaining.

2. This friendship is unhealthy and forces me to compromise my convictions.

If you chose the second statement, it is time to make a clean break. If you chose the first statement, you are ready to make amends by progressing to the next step.

Step Two: Make Meaningful Contact

You now need to determine the best way to convey the following message to your friend: "Our friendship is valuable to me, and I miss seeing you. Is there any way we can resolve what stands between us?" Knowing your friend as you do, would it be best to convey this message in writing (with a brief note), on the phone, or in person? Once you determine the means, take care to send the right message by cleaning your heart and mind of lingering desires to get back at your friend. Take a moment right now to note what has hurt you and how you may still want to get even. Be honest with yourself about your anger and feelings of revenge.

_____

_____

_____

_____

Step Three: Forgive as Best You Can

Once you have a handle on your hurt and angry feelings, you will need to do your best to step beyond them by trying to forgive. This is not an easy step, but it is vital to making amends. It begins by putting yourself in your friend's shoes and seeing the relationship and situation from his or her perspective.

• How do you imagine your friend feels about what is going on between the two of you?

_____

_____

• Is your friend feeling as hurt as you are? If so, why?

_____

_____

• If the roles were reversed, how do you think the relationship would be different?

_____

_____

• Knowing that hardly any relationship problem is ever entirely one person's fault, what do you take responsibility for in this situation?

_____

_____

• Are you able and willing to set aside your pride and give grace to your friend? If so, how can you do this?

_____

_____

Step Four: Diagnose the Problem

Once you have come to a place where you can forgive your friend and convey the simple message of wanting to make things right, the two of you may need to explore together why the problem emerged so that it won't happen again. It's up to the two of you to determine whether this step of having an honest discussion of differences is necessary.

Step Five: Rebuild Respect

This last step is critical to making amends. Ask yourself what traits your friend possesses that inspire you to become a better person and then make a list of a half dozen of your friend's most admirable qualities.

1. _____
2. _____
3. _____
4. _____
5. _____
6. _____

Now that you have made this list, you are ready to offer a sincere apology to your friend and express to him or her just how important the relationship is to you and how much you appreciate his or her qualities.

What to Do When Friends Fail

The following questions are to help facilitate a meaningful small-group discussion. Feel free to explore different territory, but don't veer too far off track. In the space provided, jot down some of the group's responses to these questions. And remember, anyone is always free to "pass" on any particular question without explanation.

1. Describe your experience of completing the exercises for this chapter. What did you learn about yourself?

_____

_____

_____

_____

2. As you consider particular friendships you have lost along the way, are there some that are more important to you than others? If so, why? What makes them valuable to you, and how do you feel about rebuilding a connection with them?

_____

_____

_____

_____

3. What do you think about the idea that what we expect from our friendships will determine whether or not those friendships can hold up under turbulent times? Think of some examples of expectations of a friend that cross the line. How do you determine that?

_____

_____

_____

_____

4. The chapter points out that most friendships fail because of one of three things: positive or negative change in one person's life, neglect of the relationship, or blatant betrayal that is either intentional or unintentional. As you consider your own failed friendships, what can the cause tell you about finding a "cure"?

_____

_____

_____

_____

5. How can you personally determine whether a broken relationship should be repaired or not? In other words, how do you decide if your differences are truly irreconcilable or not?

_____

_____

_____

_____

6. When it comes to the practical side of mending a broken relationship with a friend, which of the five steps suggested in this chapter (count the cost, make contact, forgive, diagnose the problem, and rebuild respect) would be most difficult for you to take and why? What could you do to make taking this step a bit easier?

_____

_____

_____

_____

What to Do When Friends Fail

To explore more of what the Bible has to say about this topic consider the following passages:

- Psalm 55:12–14 and 20–21 describe David's shock over a betrayal by his close friend.

  _____

  _____

  _____

- Galatians 6:1–5 talks about bearing with the failures of our friends.

  _____

  _____

  _____

- The short book of Philemon encourages reconciliation of friendship after experiencing a difficult conflict.

  _____

  _____

  _____

Other books that may be of interest to you on this topic include:

- *High-Maintenance Relationships* by Les Parrott (Wheaton: Tyndale, 1996).
  Whether they be Control Freaks, Backstabbers, Gossips, Chameleons, Volcanos, Flirts, Martyrs, or Critics, here you will find practical suggestions and advice to help you understand and cope with difficult friendships. Take the self-test in the first chapter to pinpoint what kind of relationship you are dealing with and then find dozens of practical suggestions for making immediate improvements.

- *Safe People* by Henry Cloud and John Townsend (Grand Rapids: Zondervan, 1995).

If you are wondering why you sometimes choose the wrong people to be your friends, this book will offer an explanation. It will also help you learn about things within yourself that jeopardize your relational security. On a very practical level, Cloud and Townsend will offer solid guidance for making safe choices in relationships by helping you identify nurturing people. This is a book of encouragement and hope.

• *Hope When You're Hurting* by Larry Crabb and Dan Allender (Grand Rapids: Zondervan, 1996).

Where do you turn when a friend has let you down? Do you go to a counselor? Drs. Crabb and Allender point the way as they pose four key questions hurting people need to ask: What's wrong? Who can help? What will the helper do? and What can I hope for? This book will provide guidance, choices, and hope for dealing with the pain of a friend who has failed you.

exercises

for

chapter six

Falling in Love
Without Losing
Your Mind

What's Your Love I.Q.?

This exercise will take about five or ten minutes. If you honestly answer the following items, you will have a clearer understanding of your "love smarts."

Would you say that you choose love or that love chooses you?

Love Chooses Me   *I Choose Love*

1   2   3   4   5   6   7

Are you likely to date almost anyone rather than to go without a date at all?

Almost Anyone   *Go Without*

1   2   3   4   5   6   7

Do you have a clear understanding of what qualities and character traits you want in the person you date, or are you more likely to discover that along the way?

Discover It Along the Way   *Know What I Want*

1   2   3   4   5   6   7

Do you tend to make decisions based more on the way you feel or on the way you think?

Feeling   *Thinking*

1   2   3   4   5   6   7

If a person you are physically attracted to holds values and convictions that blatantly conflict with yours, are you more likely to explore the dating relationship or move on?

Explore   *Move On*

1   2   3   4   5   6   7

If you really like the person, but after a few dates he or she show signs of disrespecting you, are you able to see what's going on and let that person know it, or are you more likely to keep quiet and put up with it?

Keep Quiet and Put Up With It   *See It and Talk About It*

1   2   3   4   5   6   7

When it comes to physical passion, are you able to set your own boundaries and stay under control, or are you more likely to let your date call all the shots?

Let My Date Set the Speed   *Set Boundaries and Keep Them*

| 1 | 2 | 3 | 4 | 5 | 6 | 7 |

Do you believe in love at first sight or slowly simmering love?

First-sight Love   *Slow-growth Love*

| 1 | 2 | 3 | 4 | 5 | 6 | 7 |

Scoring Procedure: tally your score to determine where you rank on the following level:

37–56 Above Average Love I.Q.

25–36 Average Love I.Q.

7–24   Below Average Love I.Q.

The point of this exercise is to help you assess your natural present inklings when it comes to dating relationships. Don't be discouraged by your score if it falls below average. This simply means that you may have more to gain from the principles discussed in this chapter of the book.

Are You a Good Match?

This exercise can take about five minutes and will help you determine whether the person you are dating possesses qualities and characteristics that fit the bill for you in the long run.

For each of the items in the following list, make a check mark for those qualities, traits, skills, or characteristics you possess in common with your dating partner.

Things We Have in Common

- ❑ Age
- ❑ Dependability
- ❑ Sense of humor
- ❑ Sincerity
- ❑ Religious convictions
- ❑ Family backgrounds
- ❑ Ability to adjust to things beyond your control
- ❑ Level of education
- ❑ Roles of women and men
- ❑ Political views
- ❑ Patience
- ❑ Use of alcohol and drugs
- ❑ Preference in music and entertainment
- ❑ Expression of emotions
- ❑ Management of anger
- ❑ Hobbies and activities
- ❑ Attitudes toward money
- ❑ Generosity
- ❑ Social skills
- ❑ Humility
- ❑ Hygiene standards

❑ Optimism
❑ Self-discipline and self-control

There is no numeric score for this exercise. The checklist is simply a tool for helping you see how much or how little you have in common with a person you are dating.

The True You Self-Test

This exercise will take about five minutes and will help you assess whether you are more likely to determine for yourself who you will be or whether you are more likely to be influenced by outside forces. Indicate your level of agreement for each of the following items.

1. I often feel helpless in dealing with the problems of life.

   ❏ Strongly Agree   ❏ Agree   ❏ Disagree   ❏ Strongly Disagree

2. What happens to me in the future mostly depends on me.

   ❏ Strongly Agree   ❏ Agree   ❏ Disagree   ❏ Strongly Disagree

3. I have little control over the things that happen to me.

   ❏ Strongly Agree   ❏ Agree   ❏ Disagree   ❏ Strongly Disagree

4. There is really no way I can solve some of the problems I have.

   ❏ Strongly Agree   ❏ Agree   ❏ Disagree   ❏ Strongly Disagree

5. I can do just about anything I really set my mind to.

   ❏ Strongly Agree   ❏ Agree   ❏ Disagree   ❏ Strongly Disagree

6. Sometimes I feel that I'm being pushed around in life.

   ❏ Strongly Agree   ❏ Agree   ❏ Disagree   ❏ Strongly Disagree

7. There is little I can do to change many of the important things in my life.

   ❏ Strongly Agree   ❏ Agree   ❏ Disagree   ❏ Strongly Disagree

The preceding items are designed to measure how much you have a sense of mastery and control over your life. Agreement with items 2 and 5 and disagreement with the remaining items indicate that you have what psychologists call an "internal locus of control"—that is, the belief that you are in control of and responsible for what happens in your life. Disagreement with items 2 and 5 and agreement with the remaining items indicate an "external locus of control"—the belief that what happens to you is determined by chance and that you are not responsible. These items cannot be considered the definitive test of your locus of control, but they can help you think about your own sense of taking responsibility and being true to yourself.

While the desire to be something or someone you are not may be tempting when trying to woo someone, it almost always spells disaster. For this reason, a stronger internal locus means you are more likely to be true to yourself.

Determining Your Bottom Line

This exercise will take about ten minutes and will help you uncover what you will and will not live with in a dating relationship. Take a moment to respond to each of the following questions. And remember, everyone's bottom line is different. So don't answer for anyone else but yourself.

When it comes to common courtesy from your dating partner, what do you expect?

_____

_____

_____

When it comes to seeing other people during different stages of a dating relationship, where do you draw the line?

_____

_____

_____

When it comes to expressing physical intimacy, where do you draw the line?

_____

_____

_____

When it comes to personal values, religious beliefs, and spirituality, where do you draw the line?

_____

_____

_____

Falling in Love Without Losing Your Mind

The following questions are to help facilitate a meaningful small-group discussion. Feel free to explore different territory, but don't veer too far off track. In the space provided, jot down some of the group's responses to these questions. And remember, anyone is always free to "pass" on any particular question without explanation.

1. Describe your experience of completing the exercises for this chapter. What did you learn about yourself?

_____

_____

_____

_____

2. In specific terms, how would you describe the emotions surrounding infatuation and falling in love? Are they the same thing?

_____

_____

_____

3. Journalist Helen Rowland said, "Falling in love consists merely in uncorking the imagination and bottling the common sense." In what ways does falling in love impair our judgment and deplete our common sense?

_____

_____

_____

_____

4. Do you agree that detecting your partner's values can be one of the smartest moves you make while dating? Why or why not? If you believe it is important, how do you go about discovering them?

_____

_____

_____

_____

5. How have you tried to change another person to please you more? And how have you tried to change yourself to please another person? In both cases, what was the result?

_____

_____

_____

_____

6. What "bottom lines" have you determined for yourself in dating other people? Do you need to communicate them to the person you are dating? If so, how do you do this?

_____

_____

_____

_____

Falling in Love
Without Losing Your Mind

To explore more of what the Bible has to say about this topic, consider the following passages:

- Genesis 29:18 tells the story of Jacob falling in love with Rachel.

_____

_____

_____

_____

- Judges 16 shows the serious consequences of Samson losing his mind as he falls in love with Delilah.

_____

_____

_____

_____

- Song of Solomon 8:6–7 talks about the powerful experience of being in love.

_____

_____

_____

_____

Other books that may be of interest to you on this topic include:

- *Finding the Love of Your Life* by Neil Clark Warren (Colorado Springs: Focus on the Family, 1992).

This book provides proven principles to help you choose the right person to marry. More specifically, it will show you how to eliminate the seven most prevalent causes of faulty mate selection, how to develop a clear mental image of your spouse, how to let passionate love mature before you decide to marry, how to clear conflict from the road of love, and how to celebrate your marriage with the full support of family and friends.

- *Keeping the Love You Find* by Harville Hendrix (New York: Pocket Books, 1992).

    Even the most well-adjusted people can have unresolved conflicts that make them seek out unsuitable romantic partners, unwittingly sabotage their relationships, and run from commitment without ever knowing why. This book will help you to start off your next relationship in a healthful manner and keep you loving for a lifetime.

exercises
for
chapter seven

Sex, Lies,
and the
Great Escape

Your Most Important Sex Organ

This exercise can take as little as five minutes. But take your time to give serious consideration to the questions it poses.

Most people who "lose control" in the heat of the moment blame it on their hormones. "There's nothing I could have done to restrain myself," they say. What do you think? On the following scale rate how much control you think we human beings have over our sexual activity.

Total Control   *No Control*

  1   2   3   4   5   6   7   8   9   10

If you circled 2 or higher, how do you explain your answer? Do you really believe that in a romantic relationship there comes a point where a couple simply can no longer control their physical attraction? That it is beyond their capacity to sexually restrain themselves? If you believe this, how do you substantiate your position?

_____

_____

_____

_____

Experts agree that human beings do have the capacity to be in total control of their sexual urges. Thanks to the cortex of our brain, we are different from animals. We can make decisions that govern how we will behave. With this in mind, consider what you can do personally to turn on your brain power when you are faced with a strong temptation to give in to sexual urges. Be as specific and as practical as possible.

_____

_____

_____

_____

If you are comfortable sharing your ideas with another person, compare them with someone of the same gender.

The Bonds That Bind

This exercise will take about ten minutes. Emotional bonding—if it is to be healthy and long lasting—systematically progresses through some predictable stages. Research has revealed that the reason many relationships don't last is because the foundation for bonding is too often short-circuited. Take a moment to examine the following stages of physical intimacy:

1. Eye to body
2. Eye to eye
3. Voice to voice
4. Hand to hand
5. Hand to shoulder
6. Hand to waist
7. Face to face
8. Hand to head
9. Hand to body
10. Mouth to breast
11. Touching below the waist
12. Intercourse

As you review this progression of physical bonding, make note of how far your most intimate relationships have gone and how long it took you to get there. What were the consequences? You probably don't want to write down such personal information in this workbook, but you may want to jot down a few general thoughts on how moving prematurely through any of these stages may result in unhealthy consequences for a relationship. You might consider using a metaphor in articulating your thoughts (e.g., skipping a stage is like leaving a brick out of a foundation).

_____

_____

_____

Ideally, how quickly (or slowly) do you personally think couples should progress through each stage? Make some notes next to each of the above stages.

Do you have some thoughts on what might happen in any of these particular stages if they are experienced too quickly or even skipped altogether?

_____

_____

_____

Drawing the Line

This exercise will take about ten minutes and will help you answer some of the most important relationship questions you will ever ask. Where do you draw the line? Do you only kiss before getting married? Do you do anything as long as you both keep your pants on? What have you decided is right for you, and how do you stick to your decision? To help you explore and set boundaries in your intimate relationships, review the physical intimacy scale you read about in the book:

The Physical Intimacy Scale

1. Embracing and hand holding
2. Cuddling and gentle caressing
3. Polite kissing on the lips
4. Passionate total mouth kissing
5. Intense and prolonged total mouth kissing
6. Fondling breasts and genitals outside the clothes
7. Fondling breasts and genitals under the clothes
8. Oral or genital stimulation to orgasm outside the clothes
9. Oral or genital stimulation to orgasm under the clothes
10. Genital intercourse

Again, you may not want to write this information here, but think about these questions. Where do you draw the line? Why?

_____

_____

_____

_____

What are the consequences of where you draw the line for you and your relationship (e.g., do you risk shutting off your sexuality completely; are you playing with fire; are you making intercourse inevitable)?

_____

_____

_____

_____

Once you have given this some thought and made a careful decision, consider what you will need to do to keep from crossing that line. This is a critically important step—and couples will get into trouble if it is not taken. So what practical things can you do to be sure you stick to your decision? What behaviors and what places do you need to avoid? What can you do in place of the risky behaviors? Consider a variety of scenarios and be as specific as possible.

_____

_____

_____

_____

_____

_____

_____

exercise twenty-eight

Healing the Hurt of Sexual Regret

This exercise will take fifteen minutes or longer and is designed exclusively for readers who have made unhealthy sexual decisions and need to recover from the consequences. This may be a difficult exercise, but it is crucial to helping you find healing and getting a fresh start.

First, you need to recount in specific terms exactly what pain and hurt you carry with you from having sex-too-soon. What troubles you most about your experience? If you don't want to write in this book, find another place where you can record your feelings.

_____

_____

_____

Once you have identified your heartache, you will need to take several steps to find your freedom from regret and pain. One of the best action plans we know of is found in Dick Purnell's book _Free to Love Again_ (Thomas Nelson, 1989). Here are the steps he recommends:

1. Accept God's forgiveness.
2. Forgive yourself.
3. Expect powerful changes.
4. Guard your mind.
5. Dissolve immoral relationships.
6. Purify your passions.
7. Focus your future.

From the above list, which steps would seem to trip you up most and why?

_____

_____

_____

Of course, a brief exercise in a workbook is not going to restore your spirit and erase your sexual regrets. This is only a start. Healing is always a process that takes time. So give yourself permission to be patient as you grieve and heal. In fact, we also recommend that you find someone—perhaps a trusted friend, a pastor, or a counselor—who can review the steps toward healing with you. Who could you turn to and trust with your story?

_____

_____

_____

Don't put off this part of the plan. Having a competent confidant in this process is essential to helping you move beyond your pain and get a fresh start. You can get rid of guilt and find personal renewal.

group discussion
on chapter seven

Sex, Lies, and the Great Escape

The following questions are to help facilitate a meaningful small-group
discussion. Feel free to explore different territory, but don't veer too far off
track. In the space provided, jot down some of the group's responses to these
questions. And remember, anyone is always free to "pass" on any particular
question without explanation.

1. Describe your experience of completing the exercises for this chapter.
   What did you learn about yourself?

   _____

   _____

   _____

   _____

2. On a one-to-ten scale, with one being "none" and ten being "a lot," how
   much control do you think we have over our sexual impulses and why?

   _____

   _____

   _____

   _____

3. Think back to the "compulsion for completion" concept discussed in chapter 1. How do you see this at play when it comes to our sexuality? How
   does our desire to be whole affect our sex lives? Does it differ for men and
   women, and if so, how?

   _____

   _____

   _____

   _____

4. Considering the five fundamental choices we have when it comes to having sex, which one makes the most sense to you and why? Have you, or do you know others who have fallen for unhealthy choices (e.g., "if we're in love it can't be wrong")? Why are these choices so seductive?

_____

_____

_____

_____

5. What do you think about the whole idea of drawing a line when it comes to sexual behavior on a date? Is it reasonable to think that a couple can make a decision about how far they will go and then stick to it when the heat is on? Why or why not?

_____

_____

_____

_____

6. If you were explaining to another person a few good reasons to save sex for marriage, what would you say? What would you say to the person who was no longer a virgin and was wondering whether he could reclaim his sexual purity?

_____

_____

_____

_____

Sex, Lies, and the Great Escape

To explore more of what the Bible has to say about this topic, consider the following passages:

- 1 Corinthians 6:18–20 talks about the painful impact of unwise sexual involvement in relationships.

_____

_____

_____

_____

- Galatians 5:19–21 talks about the emptiness of self-centered sexuality.

_____

_____

_____

_____

- Song of Solomon 1:1–4 celebrates the joy of sex.

_____

_____

_____

_____

Other books that may be of interest to you on this topic include:

- *Addicted to "Love"* by Stephen Arterburn (Ann Arbor: Vine Books, 1991).
  Like drug addicts or alcoholics, "love" addicts get high from sex and romance, develop a tolerance for it, and need ever-greater doses to keep going. This book examines why this addiction is on the rise, what it looks like, who it afflicts, and what you can do if you are suffering from it.

- *Sex for Christians* by Lewis B. Smedes (Grand Rapids: Eerdmans, 1976, 1994).

  Considered one of the definitive statements on sex and sexuality from a Christian perspective, this book offers frank yet compassionate discussion that is at once refreshingly open-minded and strongly biblical. Smedes treats specific sexual issues for single persons, presenting plain-spoken yet responsible perspectives on such things as erotic fantasies, petting, and adultery.

- *Free to Love Again* by Dick Purnell (Nashville: Thomas Nelson, 1989).

  The battle for a purified life can be won, and this book shows you how. It deals compassionately, yet realistically, with the sensitive issues of wrong moral choices and gives powerful advice for personal renewal. You will discover the process of healing and guidelines for a healthy love relationship by following the "seven steps to freedom."

exercises

for

chapter eight

How to
Break Up
Without
Falling Apart

Is It Time to Break Up?

This exercise will take about ten minutes and will help you determine whether breaking up is a good idea in your situation.

The following list of reasons could all be arguably justifiable for causing a breakup. Take a moment to review these reasons and place a check mark next to any that apply to you and your relationship.

It may be time to break up if . . .

_____ The relationship is stifling you.

_____ The relationship is out of balance.

_____ You can't be yourself.

_____ You feel dominated and controlled.

_____ You've outgrown each other.

_____ You feel betrayed by his or her actions.

_____ You're more interested in someone else.

_____ Your values clash.

_____ You are waiting for your dating partner to change.

_____ This person doesn't help you become the kind of person you want to be.

_____ You don't feel physically safe around this person.

_____ You don't feel emotionally safe around this person.

_____ You give more than you receive in the relationship.

_____ You feel disrespected by this person.

_____ Your dating partner is involved in unhealthy behavior (e.g., drug abuse).

_____ You feel pressured by him or her to be someone you're not.

If you checked one or more of the items in this list, you need to carefully consider whether it is time to break up and move on. Consulting with an objective friend or counselor may help you clarify your thinking and make up your mind.

Making a Clean Break

This exercise will take about ten minutes and will help you clarify your own thinking on initiating a breakup.

Consider the situation: You've dated this person for more than a year and have discovered that your values clash and that you are feeling stifled by the relationship. You want to break up. From the following options, which response would you most likely choose?

____ "What do you think about us just being friends?"

____ "I really like you, but I need some time to think about our relationship."

____ "I'm not comfortable in this relationship anymore and think it's better if we don't see each other."

The choice you made—understandably forced—in the above scenario may give you a quick glimpse into your general predisposition toward breaking up. If you chose the first response you are probably most likely to skirt the issue and end up with a painful, drawn-out breakup. If you chose the second response, you are probably aware of what you need to do but very hesitant to make a clean break. The final choice, though difficult to say, is probably the one that helps both of you make a clean break and move on.

Whatever your choice in the above situation, the following questions will help you explore issues that may give you personal insight into making you a better "breaker-upper."

What is your biggest fear about initiating a breakup?

_____

_____

_____

Considering your situation, what is your idea of an ideal breakup? What would you say and how would it turn out?

_____

_____

_____

Avoiding the Blame Game

This exercise will take about ten minutes and will help you assess the degree to which you may be blaming yourself for your breakup. Consider each of the following statements and use the scale to indicate how often each represents your thoughts. Take your time and be as honest as you can.

1 — Rarely or none of the time
2 — A little of the time
3 — Some of the time
4 — A good part of the time
5 — Most or all of the time

____ I believe I could have done a lot more to prevent the breakup.
____ I believe I am responsible for the breakup.
____ I worry about what this person thinks of me.
____ I need to take a hard look at myself.
____ I feel ashamed as a result of the breakup.
____ I detest myself for allowing the breakup to happen.
____ I think that if I changed I could win this person back.
____ I blame myself for the breakup.
____ I keep thinking about how I could have done things differently.
____ I wish I could turn back time and do things differently.

Total Score x 2 = ____

Scoring: Add up your item scores and multiply your total by two. This provides a possible maximum score of up to 100. Use the following to interpret your score.

90–100 You are wracked with feelings of self-blame and punishment over being "rejected" by this person. You could probably benefit from help from a professional counselor to help you see reality more objectively in order to move beyond your pain.

80–89 You may not be in immediate need of professional help, but you aren't out of the danger zone. You need to process your feelings with a trusted friend or counselor and recognize the potential you have to suffer from serious self-punishment.

10–79 You are on your way to escaping the guilt trap. While your twinges of self-punishment are no doubt painful, you are most likely experiencing the common and natural feelings that many have after suffering a breakup. You will want to take special care not to allow self-blame to fester when it does appear.

Moving On

This exercise can take about ten minutes to much longer, and it will help you move beyond your grief of experiencing your breakup.

Take a moment to review the section of this chapter in the book that outlines Elisabeth Kübler-Ross's steps of grief and loss. In the space provided below, note how you have or are experiencing each phase. Write about your feelings during these times, and note some specific examples of what you experienced during each of them.

Denial

_____

_____

_____

_____

Anger

_____

_____

_____

_____

Bargaining

_____

_____

_____

_____

Depression

_____

_____

_____

_____

Acceptance

_____

_____

_____

_____

How to Break Up
Without Falling Apart

The following questions are to help facilitate a meaningful small-group discussion. Feel free to explore different territory, but don't veer too far off track. In the space provided, jot down some of the group's responses to these questions. And remember, anyone is always free to "pass" on any particular question without explanation.

1. Describe your experience of completing the exercises for this chapter. What did you learn about yourself?

    _____

    _____

    _____

2. What have you learned from watching others go through breakups? What have you witnessed that seemed to make sense, and what would you say would be good to avoid?

    _____

    _____

    _____

3. Can you think of a time when you stayed in an unhappy relationship (of any kind) because of the security it provided? What allowed you to finally move on?

    _____

    _____

    _____

4. As the initiator of a breakup, what would you do to make the split less painful for the person you are leaving?

_____

_____

_____

5. As the person on the receiving end of a breakup, what would you personally do to keep your self-esteem intact?

_____

_____

_____

6. Of all the phases one can expect to experience after a breakup (denial, anger, bargaining, depression, and acceptance), which one do you think is most important and why?

_____

_____

_____

How to Break Up
Without Falling Apart

To explore more of what the Bible has to say about this topic, consider the following passages:

- Psalm 34:18 tells of God's compassion for the brokenhearted.

_____

_____

_____

- Psalm 69:20 voices the anguish of feelings that no one understands the pain of a broken heart.

_____

_____

_____

- Psalm 102:23–28 tells of God's consistency even when everything else seems to be changing.

_____

_____

_____

Other books that may be of interest to you on this topic include:

- *Seven Secrets of a Healthy Dating Relationship* by Les Parrott (Kansas City: Beacon Hill, 1995).

  Whether you are looking for someone to date, already in a relationship, or even considering marriage, this book reveals seven powerful ways for both becoming a healthy person and finding the kind of person who can help you build a healthy relationship. This book reveals qualities you probably never even thought to look for in a dating partner. Each chapter is accompanied by a self-test that will reveal how well you are doing in pursuing some of the things that matter most for a successful dating relationship.

- *Love's Unseen Enemy* by Les Parrott (Grand Rapids: Zondervan, 1994).

    Too often efforts to build loving relationships are unwittingly sabotaged by an unseen enemy: guilt. Whether you are the heartbreaker or the brokenhearted in a "former" relationship, it's not unlikely that you are struggling with the emotion of guilt. It's almost inevitable. So if you are feeling a pinch on your conscience, this book will help you identify your "relationship style" and resolve the shame and self-punishment you may be experiencing.

Relating
to God
Without
Feeling Phony

Honest-to-Goodness Doubt

This exercise will take about ten minutes and will help you consider your faith and the degree to which you struggle with doubt. On the following continuums, circle the number that indicates where you stand. Be as honest in your responses as you can be.

My "faith" is nonexistent.   My faith is rock solid.

1   2   3   4   5   6   7   8   9   10

I don't know God.   I know God personally.

1   2   3   4   5   6   7   8   9   10

The Bible is just another book.   The Bible is a holy book inspired by God.

1   2   3   4   5   6   7   8   9   10

Jesus was simply an historical figure.   Jesus is my personal Savior.

1   2   3   4   5   6   7   8   9   10

God doesn't hear my prayers.   God hears and answers my prayers.

1   2   3   4   5   6   7   8   9   10

As you consider where you stand on the above continuums, take a moment to summarize your faith in a single sentence.

_____

_____

Now take a moment to summarize your doubt in a single sentence.

_____

_____

Will the Real God
Please Stand Up?

This exercise can take about ten minutes and will help you uncover any misconceptions or distorted beliefs you have about God. Take a moment to review the passage in this chapter that ponders the question "Who is God?" Consider the four distorted concepts of God that are mentioned and indicate how often you view God in these ways.

	Rarely	Sometimes	Often
The Referee God	___	___	___
The Grandfather God	___	___	___
The Scientist God	___	___	___
The Bodyguard God	___	___	___

From the above list of distortions, which one are you most likely to view and why? If none of these four distortions is likely to trip you up, how do you sometimes misunderstand God's character?

_____

_____

_____

Now consider what may be one of the most difficult questions you have ever pondered: Who is God to you? Take a moment to write a brief paragraph on this topic. Consider the traits and qualities that come to mind when you think about who God is.

_____

_____

_____

_____

_____

_____

_____

exercise thirty-five

Does God Really Love Me?

This exercise will take about ten minutes and will help you assess the degree to which you experience God's love at a personal level. Consider each of the following statements and use the scale to indicate how often each represents your beliefs. Take your time and be as honest as you can.

        1 — Rarely or none of the time
        2 — A little of the time
        3 — Some of the time
        4 — A good part of the time
        5 — Most or all of the time

____ I believe that nothing could ever separate me from God's love.

____ I am aware of how special I am to God.

____ I believe that God is love.

____ God's grace permeates my life.

____ I'm confident that God loves me so much that he sacrificed his only Son in my place.

____ I believe God loves me as if I were the only person on earth.

____ I am free from irrational guilt feelings because of God's love.

____ I believe I can do nothing to earn God's love because it is given freely.

____ I know God loves me.

____ I can love others because God first loved me.

Total Score x 2 = ____

Scoring: Add up your item scores and multiply your total by two. This provides a possible maximum score of up to 100. Use the following to interpret your score.

90–100 You have a solid and secure understanding of how much God loves you.

80–89 You may experience some ambivalence at times about how much God loves you, but deep down you rest in knowing that he does love you.

10–79 You are struggling to know whether God loves you or not. If your score is below 60, you would certainly benefit from counsel on God's grace.

exercise thirty-six

Really Relating to God

This exercise can take as little as ten minutes to much longer, and it is designed to help you formulate how you relate to God and how you wish you related to God—and what you can do to move in that direction. This final workbook exercise may appear relatively simple at first, but it is probably the most difficult of all.

In a single sentence, summarize your faith journey and how it has brought you to your present relationship with God. Then note a few key descriptors of your present relationship with God.

_____

_____

_____

_____

Now, take a moment to consider how you might represent your present relationship with God by drawing a simple picture of it. Be as creative as you like.

Once you have completed your pictorial representation of this relationship, consider what you would like to change to make it more like the relationship you long for. What would those changes involve?

_____

_____

_____

_____

What can you do, in practical terms, to make that kind of relationship with God a reality?

_____

_____

_____

_____

Relating to God
Without Feeling Phony

The following questions are to help facilitate a meaningful small-group discussion. Feel free to explore different territory, but don't veer too far off track. In the space provided, jot down some of the group's responses to these questions. And remember, anyone is always free to "pass" on any particular question without explanation.

1. Describe your experience of completing the exercises for this chapter. What did you learn about yourself?

   _____

   _____

   _____

   _____

2. Does doubt have any place in an authentic relationship with God? Why or why not? Do you believe that God can help a person find a faith of her own? If so, how?

   _____

   _____

   _____

   _____

3. The chapter mentions a few misperceptions people often have about who God is. Do you identify with any of these? If so, how? If not, what misperceptions of God's character have you experienced?

   _____

   _____

   _____

   _____

4. If someone were to ask you why a person needs God, what would you say and why?

_____

_____

_____

_____

5. In specific terms, how do you see God as the only one who can truly fulfill our compulsion for completion? If you don't agree with this position, why not?

_____

_____

_____

_____

6. What does it mean to you when this chapter says the only way to relate to God without feeling phony is to do so with integrity? What does integrity mean to you?

_____

_____

_____

_____

Relating to God
Without Feeling Phony

To explore more of what the Bible has to say about this topic consider the following passages:

• Ephesians 3:16–19 talks about the experience of knowing God deeply.

_____

_____

_____

• Psalm 139 talks about the intimate way God knows us.

_____

_____

_____

• John 15:1–15 talks about the intimate relationship we have with God through Christ.

_____

_____

_____

Other books that may be of interest to you on this topic include:

• *The Jesus I Never Knew* by Philip Yancey (Grand Rapids: Zondervan, 1995).
    This award-winning book takes an honest look at the Jesus described in the Gospels and brings the author to conclude: "The Jesus I got to know in writing this book is very different from the Jesus I learned about in Sunday school. In some ways he is more comforting; in some ways more terrifying." Yancey offers a new and different perspective on the life of Christ. Covering everything from the manger in Bethlehem to the cross in Jerusalem, Yancey presents a complex character who generates questions

as well as answers, and a disturbing and exhilarating Jesus who wants to radically transform your life and stretch your faith.

- *Finding God* by Larry Crabb (Grand Rapids: Zondervan, 1993).

  In today's psychological culture, according to Crabb, we have become a people more concerned with solving our problems than finding God. But solving problems is not the point. In fact, whenever we place higher priority on solving our problems than on pursuing God we miss out on our relationship with him. With this book, Dr. Crabb upsets the cozy Christianity of the modern believer. He reveals anew God's top priority: not your comfort and gratification, but his glory.

- *The God You're Looking For* by Bill Hybels (Nashville: Nelson, 1997).

  To find God, according to Bill Hybels, you'll first need to put aside the caricatures, the fears, the lies, and the misconceptions that have been gathered over the centuries about who God really is. Understanding the true personality and nature of God can make ordinary people extraordinary and weak people strong. With penetrating insights and pointed anecdotes, Hybels reveals God for who he really is: A God who feels your joy and sadness, a God who doesn't stop giving, a God who has your life in his loving hands.

Becoming Soul Mates

Cultivating Spiritual Intimacy in the Early Years of Marriage

Les & Leslie Parrott

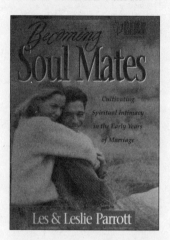

Every couple has a restless aching, not just to know God individually but to experience God together. But how? How do you really allow God to fill the soul of your marriage?

Becoming Soul Mates gives you a road map for cultivating rich spiritual intimacy in your relationship. This unique and insightful devotional helps you dig deep for a strong spiritual foundation for your marriage. It includes 52 practical weekly devotions to help you and your partner grow closer than you've ever imagined.

Hardcover 0-310-20014-8
Softcover 0-310-21926-4

Pick up a copy today at your favorite bookstore!

GRAND RAPIDS, MICHIGAN 49530 USA

WWW.ZONDERVAN.COM

Meditations on Proverbs for Couples

Previously published as *Like a Kiss on the Lips*

Les & Leslie Parrott

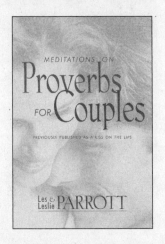

Drs. Les and Leslie Parrott know that wisdom is the bedrock of a healthy marriage. Great marriages are great because they're continually being shaped by wise principles—principles set forth centuries ago by Israel's wisest king, Solomon. In *Meditations on Proverbs for Couples*, the Parrotts share refreshing, down-to-earth reflections, brought home by candid vignettes from their own marriage and other true-life examples.

Filled with thought-provoking questions and meditations, *Meditations on Proverbs for Couples* is a great way to join hearts and minds while laying wisdom for the foundation of a strong, happy relationship.

Hardcover 0-310-23446-8

Pick up a copy today at your favorite bookstore!

ZONDERVAN™

GRAND RAPIDS, MICHIGAN 49530 USA

WWW.ZONDERVAN.COM

The Marriage Devotional Bible

NIV - Most Read. Most Trusted.

For All Seasons of Marriage

Drs. Les & Leslie Parrott

YOU WANT YOUR MARRIAGE TO BE THE BEST IT CAN BE—

Strong in commitment
Caring in communication
Joyous in lovemaking
United in vision

Above all, you want it to be grounded in faith. Whether you're celebrating your fifth or twenty-fifth anniversary, if you long for deep satisfying intimacy with God and with your mate, *The Marriage Devotional Bible* is for you.

KEEP YOUR MARRIAGE GOING STRONG

If you're ready for new growth and depth in your marriage, now is the time to make it happen. Use this Bible, and you'll discover that your future together can be even better than your past.

NIV Translation	Size 5 1/2" x 8 1/2"
Hardcover	0-310-90133-2
Softcover	0-310-90878-7
Burgundy Bonded Leather	0-310-91120-6

Pick up a copy today at your favorite bookstore!

ZONDERVAN™

GRAND RAPIDS, MICHIGAN 49530 USA

WWW.ZONDERVAN.COM

Joy Breaks for Couples

Devotions to Celebrate Marriage

Drs. Les & Leslie Parrott

Could your marriage use a joy break? Take one today! What *Joy Breaks* has done for women of faith, *Joy Breaks for Couples* does for you and your mate.

These crisp devotions are brief enough to read in a few minutes, but they pack wisdom that can strengthen and energize your marriage. They'll help you see yourself, your spouse, and married life through the lens of the Bible, brightening the shady places with humor.

Joy Breaks for Couples invites the two of you to savor your relationship: the things you love about it and even the things you're not so crazy about. Get ready to see the upside of the down! Here are truths you can apply today as you celebrate your friendship, your imperfections, family and home, your oneness, even in tough times, your future together, each other's gifts, and romance and passion.

The writers—well-known marriage and family counselors, authors, and speakers—share candidly the insights they've gleaned from their own marriages. Whether your marriage is new or seasoned, you can benefit from these nuggets of practical, biblical wisdom. So slow down … way down … relax—and take a short break that will bring both of you closer.

Joy Breaks for Couples will help you freshen your outlook as you count your blessings and discover new possibilities for your life together.

Hardcover 0-310-23122-1
Pick up a copy today at your favorite bookstore!

ZONDERVAN™

GRAND RAPIDS, MICHIGAN 49530 USA
WWW.ZONDERVAN.COM

Getting Ready for the Wedding

All You Need to Know Before You Say I Do
Les & Leslie Parrott

How do we know when we're ready for marriage? What's the secret to having a great engagement? How can we get married without drowning in debt? Where better to turn for answers than those who have gone before—experts in the area of marriage, relationships, and finance who know from experience what it takes to make the days leading up to the wedding (and the years that follow) a success!

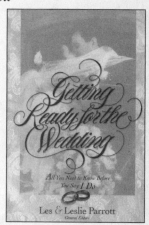

Contributions Include:

How to Know When You're Ready for Marriage—Les & Leslie Parrott
Secrets to Having a Great Engagement—David & Claudia Arp
Getting Married without Drowning in Debt—Ron Blue
What to Do with Wedding Jitters—Robert & Rosemary Barnes
Making Your Wedding More Than a Ceremony—David & Jan Stoop
How to Have a Great Wedding Night—Cliff & Joyce Penner
Getting Married When Your Parents Don't Approve—John Trent
How to Handle the Wedding Bell Blues—H. Norman Wright
For Those Getting Married Again—Thom Whiteman
After the Honeymoon—Les & Leslie Parrott

Softcover 0-310-21148-4

Pick up a copy today at your favorite bookstore!

We want to hear from you. Please send your comments about this book to us in care of the address below. Thank you.

GRAND RAPIDS, MICHIGAN 49530 USA

WWW.ZONDERVAN.COM